NOT Another Piano Book:

How everything that stopped you playing like a Piano Legend so far ... shouldn't!

by Mark Deeks

NOT Another Piano Book

Copyright © 2025 Mark Deeks

ALL RIGHTS RESERVED: No part of this book may be reproduced or transmitted in any form whatsoever, electronic or mechanical, including photocopying, recording, or by any informational storage or retrieval system without the express written, dated, and signed permission from the author.

Author: Mark Deeks. Title: NOT Another Piano Book (Second edition)
ISBN: **979-8-89686-014-3**

Cover designer: Mark Deeks

NOT Another Piano Book

For more information,
Email: hello@markdeeksmusic.com
Website: www.markdeeksmusic.com

Reviews of
NOT ANOTHER PIANO BOOK

"OMG, almost finished the book and what can I say except - I gotta get me a piano - the itch I now have to scratch! I have zero experience or ability when it comes to playing the piano but after reading Mark's book I went straight out and bought my first piano. That's how comfortable the book made me feel, along with the warm and friendly advice given by the man himself, a true Piano Legend!"
(Darren Tucker, shortly before becoming a Piano Legends client!)

"'NOT Another Piano Book' is exactly that. The furthest from a staid and stuffy approach that it is possible to be! Mark has created a book, and a teaching method, for all, whether we are complete beginners, or a 'returning after 40 years' pianist. Mark outlines in an entertaining and highly informative fashion, with relevant examples, the enormous benefits to our mental health that playing the piano will bring, and then introduces the fundamental techniques we will meet, all in a continuously engaging and hugely encouraging flow.

Mark makes piano playing available to us all, whatever our musical tastes, experiences, or preferences, and throughout his book he somehow conveys a sense of being right by our side as we embark on this excellent adventure!"
(Jo Quail, internationally acclaimed composer and virtuoso cellist)

"This little book is the perfect companion to support your expectations as a complete beginner, but it has lofty guidance and realistic advice. Mark just wants to impart his infectious belief, and exudes both enthusiasm and confidence in delivering his message". **(Elaine Wilson, Piano Legends client)**

"A really great read! Highly recommend this book which gives you every possible piece of information you will need to start a very exciting piano playing journey, whatever your age!"
(Susan Thomson, Piano Legends client)

"As its' title leaves you in no doubt about, 'NOT Another Piano Book' by Mark Deeks is far from being another stiff, dry, and uninspiring 'learn to play piano' publication. Written in a really warm, personable manner, it immediately endears the reader, by firstly – and importantly - debunking some myths about learning the piano, before summarising the benefits the journey affords (stress reduction/physical/mental health), then moves onto outlining a rational for the book's teaching approach, and the requirements for getting started.

By the time you get to the 'Let's get you playing piano' chapter, the book is preaching to the proverbial choir, as you are as equally enthused as you are inspired to actually-get-started. The author's infectious ability to convey the joy of learning and playing the piano is the key reason that this publication will succeed where so many others have failed.

This is especially the case as you are guided through the book's carefully crafted practical and theoretical chapters...the simplicity and affability of the narrative is brilliant, you actually *want* to carry on learning, to turn the page and continue, you *want* to play the piano.

In summary, if you have even the vaguest notion of wanting to start playing piano, then start your journey with 'NOT Another Piano Book' as your guide, I can assure you that you will not get lost along the way".
(Dr Mark Mynett, Senior Lecturer in Music Technology and Production, University of Huddersfield)

"If you have ever even considered learning the piano, no matter what has stopped you up to now, this is the book to read".
(Roger Bolas, Piano Legends client)

"This short read gives you all the things you need to know about playing the piano but no-one ever talks about. This is very much an elementary book aimed at the complete beginner piano or keyboard player. There is a conversational style that makes for easy reading and I felt almost coached into playing by a friend rather than being taught by an expert (which he clearly is).

This book doesn't just get you started playing the piano: there is advice on buying an instrument; discussion of learning styles; and even self-help book style guidance on the benefits of piano playing. I loved the breaking down of the difficult concept of musical keys by describing them as different languages - suddenly that complexity inherent in music made so much more sense to a non-musician.

And that is the joy of this book, it will motivate you to do something you maybe thought impossible by breaking down barriers both musically and those we create ourselves; it will give you the essentials to go from absolutely nothing to playing music in a couple of hours".
(James McFetrich, Piano Legends client)

CONTENTS

Intro 10

Forget everything you think you know about playing piano 15
"I wish I could sit down at the piano and just play…"
The imaginary bucket list 18
Myth 1: You need to spend thousands of pounds on getting an instrument 22
Myth 2: You need loads of space in your house 25
Myth 3: Learning the piano takes years 28
Myth 4: You need to play scales and play classical music to play piano 30
Myth 5: You do not have time to learn to play piano 31
Here's a bonus myth - You are too old to play piano 33

The benefits of playing piano and the four different ways you can learn 35
The physical health benefits 36
The power to reduce stress and improve your mental health.............38
One to one lessons...42
Group lessons..44
Use an app 45
The other way 46

What do you need to get started 48
What should you sit on? 48
What do the pedals do?...49
How will you hear your sound? 52
Do you need any other peripherals?..55
The most important feature to look for 57

Maintenance of your instrument 60
Summary 61

Let's get you playing piano 63
Finding your way around and which note is which? 63
How should you sit and what height should things be? 67
Moving around the keyboard 69
Learning how to control your fingers 70
Which finger is which? Your first exercises - you
can not go wrong! 76
What comes next 82
Here comes your real game changer (part 1) 84
The other half of the story (The game changer part 2) 89
Where things get really exciting 90

Conclusion 96
Here's that special offer 99
Social Media Links 100

Biography 101

NOT Another Piano Book

INTRO

When I used to be a music lecturer, I would always tell my students that the number one piece of advice I could give to help them become a 'working musician' (note, not be in a famous band or a celebrity), was to make sure they were able to turn their hand to as many musical scenarios as possible, to a good standard. Whilst I totally understand the notion that it is important to not become a 'jack of all trades and master of none', musicians often need to be able to pull in income from a number of streams in order to make ends meet. Sure, sometimes you get lucky and can get well paid for parts of what you do, but these are almost always one-off events or projects, so you are always on the lookout for the next gig or hire. Therefore, if you can increase your chances of these coming your way more frequently because you are able to deliver to a wide range of clients, then you are probably going to be just fine.

As a result, I would tell them, do not just learn to play one style of music well, learn to play several. Can you write in a range of styles too? What about teaching or directing individuals, classes or groups in educational or professional settings? Make sure you can do that too. How about arranging other people's music for a variety of different instrumental line-ups and abilities, from school groups to professional orchestras? There's another potential income stream right there. I always told the students about the importance of being able to sightread new music well (playing music you have never seen before), as well as developing their musical ear so they could pick up what someone else was playing without any written music. Then there's the importance of being able to improvise. You get the idea...

So why am I telling YOU all this, as we begin a book about getting started playing piano?

Simple, really. I want you to know that when I tell you that I believe that anyone can get started playing piano, that's the voice of experience talking. I've been working professionally as a musician since the age of 15, which frighteningly is now more than 30 years ago. In that time, I've performed, taught, directed, composed, arranged, improvised, talked about and recorded in such a wide range of musical scenarios and styles, sometimes even I laugh to myself at the variety of how my career has panned out.

For example, for more than 25 years I have worked as a musical director and arranger for numerous community singing groups and choirs numbering anything from 3 to 300 singers on stage at once. Since 2018, I have had my own community singing company called Sing United, and we currently have more than 100 singers as well as our own charity, the Sing United Foundation. These singers are just ordinary people like you and me, who sing anything from classical music to music theatre, pop to heavy metal, just for fun. And speaking of heavy metal music, I have a PhD in it (yes, really), and am in two signed metal bands, Arð and Winterfylleth, the latter of which had our 2020 album 'The Reckoning Dawn' go into the UK Rock and Metal charts at number 7. Life is pretty varied.

I have taught British comedian Lenny Henry piano, worked as a musical director with Faye Tozer of Steps fame, and conducted the Royal Northern Sinfonia orchestra on several occasions. As I said, things are pretty varied. I have run choir projects for BBC, Metro Radio, and artists such as Lindisfarne, but then have also written string parts for Japanese rock band MONO. I have done orchestral arrangements of the music of Finnish heavy metal stars Sonata Arctica, have worked as a musical director on shows like West Side Story, and co-written a comedy musical with the BBC's Alfie Joey.

Did I mention things get pretty varied?

Amongst all this, I have taught hundreds and hundreds and hundreds of people to play the piano. And I believe from the bottom of my heart that I can help you too. Right now with my Piano Legends library, I help people all over the world online to play piano easier than they ever thought possible. In fact, full disclosure, at the end of this book I am going to make you a great offer on how you can learn from me right now on a deal you might not believe.

Admit it. You just went and looked for that offer didn't you? Told you it was good!

I was really lucky with my piano teacher. Harold Sadler was his name. He taught me from the age of 5 until I was 13, when he sadly died. Thankfully by the time I was 12 he had helped me to get my Grade 8 piano (which is the highest of the main grades in the examination system here in the UK), and had laid the foundations for everything that would come. Whilst he taught me classically, he was also a jazz fan who understood the importance of helping me learn to sightread, play by ear and improvise. "What tunes do you want to learn to play?" he would ask. "'Star Wars' and the theme to TV's 'Match Of The Day'" I would reply, and so he would show me how to play those tunes as well.

In truth, I was also lucky that piano playing came relatively easy to me too, and whilst I know my parents played a big role in making me do my practice, I also know deep down that I never did as much practice as I should have done. In fact, I have often wondered what could have happened if I had really buckled down!

By the time I was a teenager, I was already used to performing for friends and family, at school and was starting to get the occasional gig elsewhere. My first paid gig involved having to improvise a version of 'Auld Lang Syne' as a newly-wed couple walked into a reception room to be greeted by their guests. I found out I needed to play this about 5 minutes before it happened. I was 15, and already performing other music when the wedding coordinator came over to ask me if I could make it happen. They wanted me to fill the time from when the doors opened and the couple were announced into the room, until they reached the head table. It was a big room, with loads of guests. Nice and stately should do it. "The groom is Scottish, and is wearing a kilt, so we thought it would be nice…".

By the way, "thought it would be nice" is a code that non-musicians use to musicians that you hear thousands of times. If someone says it, it means "we have no concept as to whether what we are asking is easy or not, but we are now going to abdicate responsibility for the situation and just assume that you can do it". Trust me.

What neither the wedding coordinator nor I knew, was that the couple intended to skip in. Fast. So, when I started playing, nice and steadily when the doors opened, I quickly needed to speed up - a lot - in order to finish the tune as they reached the head table. For a 15 year-old it was a pretty stressful, split second situation to react to and deal with. And I made it happen. Because someone "thought it would be nice". And it was.

The scene was set. Anything can happen as a piano player, and it often does. In fact, before I retire, I fully intend to write a book called 'Gigs We Have Known and Loved' and spill the beans on all the stories. However all you need to do is start and, by joining me in this book, you have done just that. The problem is there are probably a range of reasons why, no matter how many years you have wanted to play piano, you have never successfully started. Or perhaps you DID start, and then something made you stop. The likelihood is that whatever has so far stopped you being able to do what you want to be able to do on this wonderful instrument, is something that we are now going to see how we can fix.

So let us get going. Firstly, I want you to forget everything you think you know about playing piano...

FORGET EVERYTHING YOU THINK YOU KNOW ABOUT PLAYING PIANO

"I wish I could sit down at the piano and just play…"

My LIFE have I heard that sentence a lot of times during my career.

And whatever the rest of the sentence is for the person saying it, you can lay money on the fact that there is a "but" coming along soon.

But I hated the lessons my parents made me go to when I was a child.
But the piano teacher I had was boring.
But we couldn't afford a piano when I was growing up.
But I don't even own a keyboard.
But I could never fit a piano in my house.
But I don't like classical music.
But it's too expensive to learn.

I could go on. You get the idea.

What has always puzzled me, is that whilst countless people have approached me over the years to tell me they love the piano as an instrument, or they love the sound of a piano, or they love a particular singer who plays piano, so many people seem to have a negative idea of what the process of being able to play piano themselves would be like. They seem to have decided that playing piano is an unobtainable pipe dream, that they are powerless to do anything about.

Interestingly it commonly has a connection to their childhood, be it an experience they had when they were younger, or something someone such as a parent or teacher said to them that the now adult has continued to accept as fact, even many years later.

When I was a kid, I wanted tropical fish. Well I actually really wanted a dog, but when my parents would not let us get one, I thought I would try for something smaller that at least did not need walking and asked if we could get some tropical fish. There was a garden centre near where we lived that had a big tropical fish section, and I used to love it when we went so that I could stand and watch the beautiful, brightly coloured fish tranquilly sauntering around those gorgeous big tanks.

Unfortunately for me, whilst my parents are great people who have been thoroughly supportive of me throughout my life, there was a lot going on in our family at the time and they did not need any extra stress. They were not convinced that young Mark could be relied on to be consistently responsible for all the regular tasks involved in looking after tropical fish. They might have been right.

Years later when I was in my mid-twenties, I was stood looking at the tropical fish in the very same garden centre near my childhood home, and my friend asked me if was going to buy one.

I said I couldn't, and my friend asked me why.

"Because…"

I realised there was no reason. I realised that all the reasons I was about to list on autopilot were the same ones that I had been repeating to myself since childhood that were all the reasons my parents had said to me: I was not allowed one, that I would not be responsible enough, the costs would soon add up, and that the fish were too hard work.

Suddenly it dawned on me that at that very moment I was stood there, there was not actually a single reason that I could not buy a tropical fish: I was an adult with my own money and my own house, I had a degree and many instrumental and teaching qualifications. Surely I could cope with the responsibility of a tropical fish?

So I walked up to the shop assistant, got out my wallet… lost my confidence and bought a goldfish!

BUT… the principle remains the same, my friends! I had spent years telling myself that something was not possible or not attainable, all based on circumstances I had experienced and accepted as the end of the story when I was a child. But things change, you change, and circumstances change.

So, what if the circumstances that have meant you have not yet played piano have changed too? What if the teacher whose lessons you hated as a child only showed you one way to play and there is another way? What if they only knew how to teach classical music so stuck to that but you love pop music? What if they had never played jazz so did not know how to show you how to improvise but someone else could? What if your teacher was great at scales but had never taught how chord sequences and the building blocks of pop songs work, and you just want to write your own music?

What if even though your childhood home did not have room for a real piano, your current home has more than enough room for a portable keyboard? What if you heard someone say learning piano was expensive when you were young, but actually as an adult you have never checked what might be involved and just assumed it would seem expensive now? What if someone told you it takes hours of practice every day to get any good at piano and you have just accepted this as fact when it is not?

Maybe it is time to forget everything you think you know about playing piano and start again with fresh eyes, because believe me when I tell you, I have had adults every age from their twenties to their eighties tell me all those things and more. Then we got them playing.

The imaginary bucket list

During 2020 I spent some time researching and asking my audience about how they viewed the concept of a 'bucket list'. I was trying to get to the core of why we ALL (myself included) talk about things we say we have always wanted to do, but then never do anything about. What particularly interested me, was the question of what form these bucket lists take for us. For example, how many of us actually have a physical bucket list on paper? Alternatively in this technology obsessed time, how many have now made digital versions of our most desired experiences and wishes? Or finally (and this struck me as the most intriguing possibility) how many of us have what we might call an 'imaginary bucket list'?

The idea that people might on the one hand say that they have ALWAYS wanted to do something, go somewhere, learn something new, or whatever it may be, then leave it to the lottery of MEMORY fascinates me. None more so because I do it too! The more I thought about it, I could not believe that if we say that these experiences are something we have wanted to do for as long as we can remember, why do we not even do the simplest of tasks and write it down. What if we forget something? Was it that important to us in the first place?

I once asked my audience on the Mark Deeks Music Facebook page about whether they had a bucket list, and gave them a choice:

1. Yes and it's written down
2. Yes but it's in my head
3. No I don't have a bucket list

The range of comments was really interesting. One responder we will call Rebecca, found the discussion caused her to re-evaluate and realise something. I'm sharing this exchange here, as I think there will be lots of you who can identify with this:

Rebecca - My bucket list is in my head but I don't call it that. It's ever changing too. Some things are already ticked off and some things now seem less important as I make my way through my life.

Mark Deeks Music - Interesting that you're conscious that it develops as you go. So what DO you call it?

Rebecca - I'm not sure that I have a name for it… or even that it's an 'it'. More of a collection of ideas in my head that I chat about with my husband. Things I and we would like to do / try / visit. I do wonder if there is a reason I don't label them as my 'bucket list' and think maybe it could be so I don't feel like I've failed if I don't 'tick them off'.

Mark Deeks Music - OK this is getting really interesting. I'm fascinated about how people perceive this stuff and how they go about doing anything about it - if at all. The fact what we CALL these things could affect whether we do them or not fascinates me.

Rebecca - That's a very interesting point. I feel like I possibly have 'ticked some things off' that I never had on my (non-labelled) bucket list. For example: if I'd thought about it before recent years, owning our lovely home and finding love may have been on there, or skydiving. It just so happens that I did those things without thinking of them as 'life goals' or items on a list.

Mark Deeks Music - Love it! Now you're talking about unconsciously ticking things off!

Rebecca - It's a curious topic... glad you made me think! When I was out running today, I realised I do have a list of goals that I do tick off and they're written down! It's not a bucket list but this discussion made me think of it - I have a list of goals for my running (like run a 5k in so many minutes etc). They're micro stepped so once I tick one off, the next one is there ready.

Obviously I am not here to convince you that you need to write down beautifully presented lists of all of the things you want to achieve or experience in your lifetime, although some of you may now feel you would like to give that a go. However, I wonder if taking a minute to be a little bit more conscious about the choices we are making in terms of a bucket list, imaginary or not, might help some of us to evaluate more clearly what is important to us, and decide what we would like to do with our time accordingly.

I asked one potential client of mine (let's call her Sally) why, if she had always wanted to play piano, why if she was now in her fifties she had never made it happen. "I didn't think it was available to me because I didn't learn when I was a child". I was really taken aback by this. Maybe forty years of wanting to play but not doing anything about it had passed on the basis of an assumption that was totally false, a myth. I did not know whether to laugh with or cry for her. What made me happy, though, was that I knew we could fix it easily. Within days Sally had taken delivery of a new piano, she was smiling, and the piano even had a nickname: Sassy Steinbach!

Now, is that client of mine ever going to become a professional piano player, touring the world, wowing fans with her piano skills? Almost certainly not (sorry Sally!). But is she now able to sit down for 15 minutes with a cup of tea and pick out a few notes here, a few chords there, a bit of a song here, a recognisable old favourite there? You bet. Even though there may be a tinge of regret at waiting all those years, I think it may even taste a little sweeter as a result. And even if what she plays is sometimes not perfect (!), it puts a smile on her face and how priceless is that?

As I specialise in helping adults like Sally start playing piano, it might not come as a surprise that there is a recurring theme of age and people thinking that they are told old to begin. I once asked some of the people who use my Piano Legends content if they had had lessons when they were a child, how many years had it been from when they stopped until they started learning with me. The range of answers was astonishing - up to 61 years, and answers of more than 40 years were common.

What struck me most was that for most of the people, the length of time was essentially their entire adult life. Decades of time when they could have had the pleasure of playing the music they loved had passed by. Of course jobs, families and other personal commitments had played their part in restricting the time people had available for their hobbies, but the dream of being able to play the piano had never left them. And for those who had been faithfully repeating something from their childhood as a reason it could never happen for them, now they knew differently, and it is so exciting to see.

I want to take you through some of the most common things people say to me when I ask them what has been stopping them taking the first step to start playing piano because it is likely that at least one of them will resonate with you too. I consider myself on a mission to break down these piano barriers for as many people as possible and get them playing with all the benefits it brings. I call them my Top 5 Myths About Learning To Play Piano. Good name, that.

Myth 1: You need to spend thousands of pounds on getting an instrument

This is just not true. Clearly I know that everyone has their own budget, and what might be expensive to you might not be expensive to the next person. But I can tell you one thing with certainty, having helped countless people over the years to buy a piano or keyboard: it absolutely does not need to cost thousands of pounds or dollars. In fact it does not even need to cost £500. In fact, the most common electric keyboards I recommend to people looking to get started are usually £250 or less, and that is new. If you start looking in the secondhand market you can probably get that down to £200 or less, maybe even £100 on a lucky day. And of course, if these figures still feel too much right now, nobody is insisting you have to have it all ready and available today. Could you put a little aside each week or month so that in a few months you can make it happen? Where there is a will there is a way and all that!

One story that should give you hope is what happened to a client of mine, we will call her Emma. I announced on my social media channels that I was going to be running a free 5 day challenge called Start Playing Piano in Just 5 Days (as you are starting to see, when naming the services

I offer, I like to be crystal clear what is involved and not go all 'woo' in my marketing!)

Whilst I told people that they could take part using an app on their phone if they really wanted to, they would have a much better experience if they had a physical instrument that they could use. However I also offered that if anyone did not know where to start trying to find one, either secondhand or new, that they should send me a private message with their town and approximate budget and I would source one for them for no charge. I know that the terminology in keyboard descriptions can, like anything you have never bought before, seem a bit intimidating, so I always offer this service to people (that includes YOU).

Emma contacted me to tell me that whilst she was desperate to take part in the challenge as this was something she had wanted to do all her life, money was tight right now as her earnings had been affected like they had for many people during the Covid-19 crisis of 2020. Before I had a chance to ask her for her location and budget, she sent me a link to a keyboard she said she had found on Facebook Marketplace near where she lived, with the simple question, "Is this worth it?"

The keyboard was TEN POUNDS!

I could not believe it. "YES Emma! Get that!"

Now in the interest of transparency and honesty, I have to be straight with you. Was this the most amazing keyboard in the world? No. It was not the best. Mind you, was it the worst I had ever seen? Not in a million years! The point was that it was a first step, something was happening. Emma was up and running, and all it took was a little action. At the time of writing, when you start to look lower than the £150-£200 range, you are starting to look at keyboards that may not be the instruments you want to play forever, but could they be ideal to get you going whilst you see if you want to make playing part of your life? Absolutely! Unfortunately I cannot promise you will find a keyboard for ten pounds like Emma did, but you get my point: you do NOT need to spend thousands of pounds to get started playing piano.

If your preference is that you would rather have an acoustic piano (that's a 'real' one, not an electric one with speakers in it), and you have the space, sadly we live in a world where people literally give them away for free regularly on all your favourite secondhand marketplaces. In this situation all you need to do is pay for the removal costs and a piano tuner when it gets to your home. As a guide, currently in the UK, assuming you are moving a piano within the same local region where you live, you might pay around £150-£250 for the removal company, and then around £60-£100 for a piano tuner. Therefore you would end up paying a similar amount as you might for your first electric piano or keyboard, but you would have a beautiful instrument aesthetically too.

A couple of pieces of advice for you if you decide to go down that route. Firstly piano removals is a specialist job, and frankly when you see it done well, practically an art form! Real acoustic pianos are extremely heavy and bulky to move, and as a result, some 'normal' furniture removal companies will refuse to move pianos, whilst some will but only if they don't involve any stairs. Yes that's right, specialist companies who do nothing but piano removals will take on moves that involve staircases, even spiral ones. Like I told you: it is an art, so if you are getting it done, make sure to ask any removal companies you speak to if they have experience of moving pianos, or just simply make sure you add the word "piano" in front of "removal companies" in your Google search!

The second key (sorry!) piece of advice is about getting a piano tuner. Unlike electric keyboards, acoustic pianos need regular maintenance. As a guide you should look to get your piano checked over once every 12-18 months on average. Once again, piano tuners are an extremely specialist job, and for the skill involved, usually very reasonably priced. As I mentioned, the actual tuning would currently tend to cost around £60-£100. Higher costs than this would usually be as a result of more significant work than just needing the tuning doing, such as strings, the hammers, felts or other parts of the internal mechanics needing replacing. Essentially think of it in a similar way to getting your car serviced: the normal maintenance checks will have a standard price, and then if your tyres or brakes need replacing you will pay extra.

Like with regular car servicing, keeping your piano in good working order is more than worth it, and stops bigger costs mounting up later on. One final piece of advice on this subject is to definitely NOT get it tuned immediately after it has been moved into its new location. Acoustic pianos are made up of a lot of wood, iron and other materials that can be affected by changes of temperature, moisture in the air, and the act of moving them itself. As a result it is always advised to wait around two weeks after the piano has been moved to let it 'settle' before getting anyone to carry out maintenance on it, otherwise it is likely to go out of tune quite quickly again afterwards and land you with another bill for a repeat visit from the tuner. Beware also, because piano tuning is such a specialist skill, there are sadly often not many of them in any one town, and as a result they often get booked up well in advance, so it is worth making a call as soon as you have an idea of when you might need them.

Myth 2: You need loads of space in your house

Well if you are wanting to buy a grand piano the like of which you might see in a concert hall, then yes, you ARE right. Sorry. The thing is, most of us do not have the room for that, but there are countless people the world over who are happily playing something else instead, so what are the solutions that overcome this myth?

Working downwards in size from a grand piano, the next option is known as a baby grand, however even these are going to still need quite a good-sized room to fit one in. As a result, if people want an acoustic piano, most commonly they go for what is known as an upright piano as they take up far less space. These are the ones that most of us think of as perhaps having seen in school.

When you are planning the space you are going to need in your house, notice that in terms of the wall space needed (the horizontal dimension, if you will), there is actually very little difference between each of these types of piano, due to them all having the same number of keys (more of that in a moment); they're all going to be approximately 5ft wide or maybe a little over depending on if there is any wood either side of the keyboard. What changes size wise, and what it means if you get an upright piano, is the depth, i.e. how far it is from where you are going to sit at it to the back of the instrument. An upright piano measures considerably less in that dimension (usually approximately only 2ft) compared to a grand piano (anything from 7-10ft deep).

For many people, rather than an acoustic piano, a more practical solution can be one of the many electronic keyboard or piano options available. Of course, like with any kind of product or service that you have never bought before, the product descriptions, specifications and terminology used can be a little intimidating at first. As we are talking about space, however, let me help you start with the basics.

A full-sized keyboard (whether electric or a piano) has 88 notes. You do also, occasionally, see keyboards with either 73 or 76 notes. If space is at a premium in your home, then that slight reduction in size needed in comparison to a full sized keyboard may make all the difference, but note these sizes are far less common, and many manufacturers do not make them at all. The smaller keyboards you might think of as having seen in school have 61 notes, and so maybe a foot or small narrower in terms of wall space (4ft or maybe a little less depending on the speaker sizes built into the keyboard).

The next most common sized keyboard is one that has just 49 notes, which are obviously smaller again, that you sometimes see people have on computer workstation desks. These are most commonly a type of what are called MIDI controller keyboards. Without worrying too much about the technology side of these, what this usually means is that the keyboard itself does not generate sounds (or therefore have speakers) and is used to control sounds produced by the computer it is connected to. Whilst these are a great, practical tool, they do not make the ideal instrument to learn how to play piano on.

Having dealt with the depth and width of potential instruments, you may have thought that they were the only dimensions that were an issue with regard to how much space you need in your house to get playing. However, the height of your set of keys can also be something to consider, even if it only makes a psychological difference to how big you 'feel' the piano or keyboard is. For example, acoustic upright pianos and their full wooden bodies, may be approximately 4ft high. Full sized electric pianos commonly come with wooden bodies as well, but may be a foot or so shorter.

Then the vast majority of electric keyboards may be only a few inches deep, but need to sit on a keyboard stand. However, whilst by the time they are sat on a stand the combined height will be several feet again, these instruments 'feel' considerably smaller. This is partly because of their lack of a wooden body (which tends to feel more like a piece of furniture), and partly because their portable nature means that they can be taken off their stand and stood on their end if more space is temporarily needed in the home.

All in all, whilst you will need a good sized room if you want a grand or baby grand piano to not 'take over' your space, many people find that they are pleasantly surprised just how easily they can fit their new instrument into their home. Once you consider the range of options available, especially the portability and flexibility of a lot of electric keyboards, you can see that there is no need to let a false idea of the space that is needed stop you getting started.

Myth 3: Learning the piano takes years

This is a myth that stems from people failing to remember the context of why most people start learning to play - and it stops them starting. In the vast majority of cases, those people with an interest in playing piano do not have a desire to become professional pianists. This is especially the case of most adults who commonly already have a career, or perhaps are even retired, and want a new hobby.

A few years ago, my wife and I decided to take up running with the plan being that we would take part in the Great North Run, the largest half marathon in the world, held annually in our home city of Newcastle upon Tyne. When we first started trying to run, we could barely make it to the end of the street without some difficulty. However, whilst we never found it easy at all, within a few months we were able to run 5k, then 10k, and eventually the half marathon within about a nine month period. Were we fast? Not at all, but was that the point? Not at all. For us the benefits were many, even without worrying about speed. We were far fitter, the running was good for our mental health, and the asthma I had had an issue with for a number of years had greatly improved.

If we had allowed ourselves to think about the ability levels of professional athletes, we might have been deterred from even having a go at running at all, because we would have been comparing ourselves in an unreasonable context. If so, we would have missed out on a huge range of potential benefits just because we were never going to be good enough to be a professional, and I think you would agree, that would have been a mistake.

Adults have a concept of finished products that children do not, and it can be a huge hindrance. Consider this: young children are entertained by the fact that they can walk up to a piano, randomly hit the keys, and get a noise out of an instrument they have no knowledge of how to play. And any of us who have seen this happen in a hotel reception or restaurant know how long they can find this fun for! Adults on the other hand simply hear noise. Why? Because they have the concept of the sound of their favourite artists or bands to compare the noise to, and it does not compare favourably! Consciously or not, this is reinforcing the feeling that to learn to play 'properly' is a process that takes years. However, this fails to take one crucial point into account.

I had been going to piano lessons for seven years before, at the age of 12, I achieved my Grade 8 from the Associated Board of the Royal Schools of Music (ABRSM), the highest of the main grades available. Then, after some more lessons, I started performing and teaching professionally aged just fifteen. However, remember, I wanted to become a professional and you, most probably, do not, and that changes everything. You want to switch off for ten minutes after a difficult day at the office. You want to unwind for fifteen minutes playing a song you love after you have put the children to bed. You want to have ten minutes a day to improve your mental wellbeing or have some precious time just for you.

Whatever the motivation is for you, this change of context changes everything, and as a result, we can remove a barrier to playing that is huge for a lot of people: you are not trying to 'learn piano'. What you are trying to do is enjoy discovering the skills needed to play the music you love well enough to de-stress and have the satisfaction and mental boost that follows, and you certainly do not need many years of lessons to be able to begin enjoying that.

Myth 4: You need to play scales and play classical music to play piano

No, no, and also no. I do not remember the last time I made someone that I help play a scale. Are scales useful? Yes. Can you learn a lot about the building blocks of music if you play them? Unquestionably. Do you NEED to play them in order to successfully be able to play your favourite song? Not in a million years.

Let us take a step back for a moment. Firstly, you might not know what a scale is, and that is absolutely fine. In basic terms, they are structured patterns of notes that are used the world over as the basis for the most common technical exercises on the vast majority of instruments, and there are hundreds and hundreds of different patterns. Part of the reason that people associate them so much with learning an instrument is that for many years, they have formed the basis for a part of most instrumental exams all over the world, and so for many they are unavoidably attached to traditional exam-based learning. Whether you have actually ever studied for one of these exams or not, a lot of people at least know someone who has, and to many of our ears they sound pretty boring. Whilst there are some people who enjoy practicing scales, I think it is safe to say that they are in the minority, and for most players they are a means to an end at best.

Once upon a time, at least as far as the UK is concerned, learning an instrument as a child usually meant that your teacher would want to enter you for one of the ABRSM exams. Whilst the pieces available for the student to choose from did usually include one or two pieces that could loosely be described as jazz or blues in nature, the vast majority of pieces you were asked to play were inherently classical. Unless you were lucky enough to find a teacher who was willing to take a different approach, this was the experience that most young players had, and therefore came to associate with what it means to learn the instrument. I firmly believe that as a result, there are still many families for whom this association is still uppermost in their mind, and so if their personal musical tastes are more popular music in nature, they conclude that learning piano would not be enjoyable, so they never start.

Do not mistake this opinion for any kind of criticism of learning to play classical music, it most certainly is not. If you would like to learn to play Bach, Debussy or Chopin, then that is great, it is doable, and you absolutely should do that. However doing that comes with a bit of a different skillset to learn, different practice tips, and probably a different timescale to take into consideration. Of course there is an overlap between learning classical and more popular music based styles, but do not make the assumption that in order to play piano you NEED to learn classical music. Nothing could be further from the truth.

Myth 5: You do not have time to learn to play piano

I have heard this literally a million times in my career. Maybe more. However, I just do not think that "I don't have time" is the real root of the issue.

Instead, I think one of several other things are causing the problem.

Perhaps you have already decided that learning the piano takes years (see myth 3!) and therefore there is no point in even starting. Or perhaps you are already playing but your method of learning is not working for you. Or perhaps (consciously or not) you are not prioritising having a little time each day just for you, to do something you love that makes you happy. You are finding other things to do that you have decided are more important at that moment because no one wants to sit down at the piano and feel like they are not getting any better, that they will never be able to do it, or that they are not as good as they want to be. You want to be motivated, excited, and pleased with what you are achieving. You want to play music that you love, not something that you feel that you are being made to. Most importantly, you want to be able to enjoy the process, not have to sit down for long hours of tedious exercises and nursery rhyme-like music.

Because most of all, this is supposed to be fun, right? This is your hobby. As I have already said, if you are wanting to train to be a professional, that changes the whole context, and we would be talking about a totally different set of boundaries and expectations. But if you want to play piano purely for fun, then it needs to be fun. This is why I teach all the players I help to call their time sat at the keyboard 'playing' not 'practice'. Even that small change of language can make a huge difference to people, because 'practice' soon equals "I don't have time" - we are only human after all. I also tell the people that I coach to only sit for ten or fifteen minutes at a time, even when they have been playing for a while. This is for a number of reasons including this being far more manageable to fit into a busy modern life that declaring you are going to find time for an hour every evening. Also, by setting these more achievable goals, psychologically you have a huge win, because you are far more likely to succeed in making it happen. I can also promise you that finding ten or fifteen minutes a day five or six days a week will see you make much better progress than doing an hour once only at the weekend.

The trick is to 'attach' these short blocks of time to something that you know is definitely going to happen. Ten or fifteen minutes when you first get up, after you have brushed your teeth, with your morning cup of coffee, when you first get in from work, after your evening meal, after you have put the children to bed, just before you go to sleep to relax, whatever works for you. If you can find time for more than one short block of time in the day then that is even better, but keep the sessions short and sweet, and motivationally leave yourself wanting more. If you really want to make the most of your time at the keyboard and make even better progress, then do what I call 'targeted practice'. Plan in advance of sitting down what you are going to do in those ten or fifteen minutes and do ONLY that. If you succeed at what you have planned in six minutes, walk away. You will be left feeling great and desperate to get back to the keyboard to have another go. If, on the other hand, you find that ten minutes was not enough to conquer what you targeted, then at least you are not going to sit there for an hour getting increasingly frustrated. Come back to it another time, another day. This is a long process, but protecting how you feel about it psychologically, your confidence, motivation and excitement is, for my money, the most important thing to look after when you are learning an instrument. Remember more than anything this is supposed to be fun, when it is fun, time flies, and we all deserve a little fun in our lives!

Here's a bonus myth - You are too old to play piano

It is a really common issue for many adults to think that they are too old to start a new hobby, especially learning piano. If I have heard this once, I have heard it a thousand times. Please be assured this simply is not the case. Remember how I told you that I once asked my Piano Legends clients how many years it had been since they had a piano lesson when they were a child. I was astonished to find that the average answer was 46 years, and the longest was an incredible 61 years. That is literally a lifetime of not playing piano when you have a desire to do so, and that makes me really sad. Can you imagine going decades wanting to do something, and denying yourself the possibility of all the pleasure and enjoyment that could bring?

You might remember me telling you earlier about one of my members Sally, who said to me that she did not think playing piano was "available" to her **because** she did not learn as a child. Imagine that. Of course, there are lots of reasons that someone may not get the opportunity to play as a child, such as a lack of financial resources in the family, parents who may have prioritised school work, and so on. But now in her mid-fifties, she had still not yet got round to doing something that she would love to do. To me, this comes back to this false idea that it takes years to learn to play piano, and we have already dealt with how this myth is built on trying to apply one context to everyone. Yes, if you are wanting to become a professional piano player, then there is a lot to learn and you have a lot of skills to master. But this lady did not want to become a professional piano player, she simply wanted to have some enjoyment, some time just for her later in life and there was absolutely no reason that we could not make this happen for her, so we did.

Hopefully by this stage you have seen that getting started playing piano may not be as impossible or intimidating as you had assumed. Perhaps you are realising that there was no reason you could not have started sooner, or at least you now feel that you are excited to get going as soon as possible. However you are currently feeling, I want you to know the news is about to get even better for you. There are actually a huge number of benefits of playing piano, that you perhaps have not even considered before. Strap in - this is about to get even more exciting.

THE BENEFITS OF PLAYING PIANO AND THE FOUR DIFFERENT WAYS YOU CAN LEARN

I am a massive believer that every single person who has ever wanted to play piano has some kind of piano 'why'. This could be any one of a hundred different reasons why you dream of being able to play this fantastic instrument. It could be as simple as the fact that you enjoy the sound of a piano. It could be because you did not get the opportunity when you were young and now you can afford to give yourself the opportunity as an adult. Perhaps you had an elderly family member who used to be able to play and entertain the family at special occasions and you want to be just like them. There will be those amongst you who would love to earn a living as a professional piano player, whilst perhaps the majority of you just want to be able to relax for a little bit of time after work as a way to unwind after a hard day's work. Some people want to learn to play one specific song that means something to them personally, whereas some people have a dream of mastering a particular style of music such as jazz. Lots of people have ambitions to become a great songwriter and see the piano as a means to help them understand how to write their own material. Then there are those who are good singers but can see the appeal and benefit of being able to accompany themselves when they perform. Perhaps you are now retired and have more time on your hands than you once did, and playing the piano is staring back at you from your bucket list, and you think "if not now, when?"

I could go on, but you see my point. All of these reasons are equally valid, but whatever your motivation is, it is important to start by asking yourself what yours is. Even if no one else knows, it does not matter. What matters is that you know, and you keep it at the forefront of your thinking, because as I said in Chapter 1, if your ambitions are as simple as being able to pick your way through a few notes, or a song you love after work to relax, that frames everything in terms of how you practice and the goals you set yourself very differently to if you want to be earning a living from it within five years.

Regardless of the starting point motivation that is personal to you, there can be no doubt that there are a considerable number of benefits of learning to play piano, both physically and mentally, and in this chapter we are going to talk about just some of them. By doing so, you can hopefully feel inspired and see that there is so much joy and reward available to you, right from the very beginning of your piano journey.

The physical health benefits

There are few names in piano playing that carry more weight than Steinway. Manufacturers of what many would consider some of the finest pianos ever made, when Steinway speak, others listen. So when they devote a page of their website to the benefits of playing piano*, you can be sure that this is well-informed advice and research.

"Research has shown that piano lessons for older adults have a significant impact on increased levels of Human Growth Hormone, which slows the adverse effects of ageing".

As I mentioned in Chapter 1, I very commonly speak to adults who are aged 50-90 who have already decided (or perhaps have spent years telling themselves) that they are too old to start. I have already told you about the lady who thought that playing piano was not "available" to her because she did not learn when she was a child. What she found more than anything, was a mindshift change was all it took to get her started enjoying her new hobby and all the benefits it brought her. For a number of years, I have had one private client who is in her eighties, who regularly refers to how part of the reason she continues to play the piano regularly is because she feels that it keeps her hands moving and as supple as possible, despite her combatting some of the common issues of ageing in terms of difficulties with joints.

The London Piano Institute, like Steinway, has an area of their website** also similarly devoted to talking about the wide range of benefits of playing, including a section on how piano can improve cognitive development:

"Numerous scientific studies have shown that playing an instrument stimulates the brain in a unique way. When playing the piano, neurological pathways are connected. These pathways can even help you in other disciplines – such as maths, science, and engineering!"

As we will see when we look at the mental health benefits of playing, this is not the only way that piano not only has a direct benefit, but also potential additional by-product advantages.

For those suffering long term with a chronic illness, playing piano can provide a huge source of comfort. Take, for example, a friend of mine we will call Dawn, who suffers from ME (Myalgic Encephalomyelitis) or Chronic Fatigue Syndrome. Her condition is one that has a wide range of recommended treatments including everything from exercise programmes to medicines and talking therapies. For Dawn, however, she describes playing piano as her preferred method of coping:

"For me, playing the piano has become a lifeline. On days where I suffer with severe brain fog, I can just sit and play. Not necessarily using any music as reading it can be draining, but just to sit and play makes me feel I've accomplished something in a day where getting out of bed is like running a marathon".

The power to reduce stress and improve your mental health

Just to be clear, I am certainly not a doctor. Although technically that is not correct as I have a Doctorate in heavy metal music (yes, really, but that is literally another book!) However, I think that stress is something we all recognise when we experience it for ourselves. In recent years, I think that we can all agree that stress has manifested itself in more ways than ever. At the time of writing in 2024, the Coronavirus pandemic of 2020 is still fresh in the memory. During the time we saw people not only worried about the virus, but also about their friends and family, they were worried about running out of money, they were worried about jobs and businesses they had spent our lives building, and so on.

All of us need to find a way to switch off from our troubles or find a way to reduce how much they affect us. We hear a lot about the importance of mental health, wellbeing, and a need to de-stress. During the summer of 2020 I did my first jigsaw and found that I LOVED it. Whilst I was very conscious that this might make me even more of a geek than my wife tells me I am, it did make me feel a little bit cooler that it was a Metallica album cover, although that is clearly open for debate! The point is that whilst I obviously LOVE music, and it is pretty much the most important thing in the world to me other than my wife and daughter (oh and my dog Herbie and the rest of the family!), it is a challenge for me to use music to switch off. I make a living from it, have lived and breathed music for as long as I can remember, and so it is pretty unavoidably at least partially labelled 'work' in my brain.

However, this does not need to be the same for you, and in fact it is very likely that it will not be. Musical hobbies help so many people by reducing stress, whether they are playing, listening to or writing their own music. Even a cursory glance at the results of a Google search for "playing an instrument to relieve stress" will show you the plethora of research out there (by people who are MEDICAL doctors!) that has come to this conclusion. In fact, I looked at some of these in my 2023 TedX talk called 'Could Heavy Metal Music Help Maintain Your Mental Health?' (which you can see here: http://tinyurl.com/tedxmarkdeeksbook). From music lessons literally being prescribed as a treatment, to countless research papers advocating musical hobbies for this kind of benefit, there can be little doubt that starting to play piano can greatly reduce your stress levels. And here comes the best bit for those of you who just want to do this for fun: there is plenty of research to say that the more seriously you approach your new hobby, the less relaxing it will be.

The key here is to have an active engagement with music. Whether playing music, singing, drumming or listening to music, they have all "been seen to improve mental health outcomes, lowering levels of both anxiety and depression".*** And if you're trying to play a new instrument, remember that the rate that you get better at the instrument IS NOT the same as the rate it does you good. Read that sentence again, I'll wait. On day 1, if you spend 10 or 15 minutes wondering where to put your fingers, or which key to press, they are 10 or 15 minutes where your brain is unable to worry about whatever is currently stressing you. Now imagine the ripple effect of making that a regular habit.

The discussion surrounding mental health has thankfully become much more prominent in recent years. Where once there was a tendency (especially amongst men) to suffer in silence, refuse to discuss any problems, and certainly never admit it in public, we now see open discussion, debate, and a huge variety of opportunities for people to get the support they need. Furthermore, a greater tendency to be aware of the importance of protecting our mental health has meant that an increasing number of people are looking to a wide range of hobbies and pastimes to alleviate, or indeed prevent, mental health issues. Music-based hobbies are, of course, excellent methods of doing just this, whether listening to, playing, or writing. At least in part, this is often to do with the fact that for the majority of people music is unrelated to their day to day tasks, responsibilities or careers.

Take for example, a client of mine we shall call Andrew, who is a doctor:

"For me the benefits of playing include having a focus, the enjoyment of learning something new, having a positive distraction from slumping in front of the TV, and demonstrating to the children that learning a skill is enjoyable and possible even in your 40s, are all good for my mental health".

What I really love about Andrew's example is that not only does he perceive a number of direct mental health benefits for himself, but he also is able to pass indirect benefits on to others in the form of his children by using his learning piano as an example to them of positive things that can be achieved. He went on:

"I've always found that making music (especially for someone like me who is not artistic in the general sense) has a particular transcendent quality that is soothing to the soul and promotes mindfulness".

Having spent my life working extremely closely with music in many forms, it is refreshing for me to hear how someone from a scientific background is able to identify the positive feelings and effects of playing music, in a way that it may be that I am sometimes too close to music to recognise. What should encourage you, is that (by his own admission!) Andrew is no piano expert! Whilst he regularly acknowledges how he has noticed improvements in his playing and understanding during his time learning from me, I know that he would happily tell you that he still considers himself a beginner player. Despite this, he is able to identify and enjoy this huge range of mental health benefits, which of course suggests that you should not assume that the mental boost is directly correlated to your practical abilities on the keys!

He is not alone. Within only a matter of a week or so of becoming a client, a lady called Fiona felt the benefits were already identifiable, not just in how she feels when she plays, but also what happens as a result of it:

"Playing the piano helps me to relax after a long day at work. After I've put the kids to bed, I like to sit at the piano with my coffee and it's MY time. It gives me something to focus on and is my way of taking the stress out of the day. I'm convinced that I sleep better since I've been playing in the evening too!"

How amazing is that? Not only a pleasurable, relaxing way to spend an evening, and a recognition of the importance of having some time just for you, but also as a by-product, a better night's sleep! And of course it is well established how beneficial for us all a good night's sleep is, both mentally and physically.

It is also common to hear stories about other kinds of resulting benefits. In October 2020, I posted in a large public Facebook group made up of adults who have an interest in learning piano, to ask for contributions from people who felt they could relate playing piano to a mental health benefit of some kind. One particularly moving response from a lady called Stephanie was this:

"I started taking lessons during one of the most stressful times in my life. The joy of playing sustained me. I say to my husband, 'In a way, it saved my life'. The joy of piano motivates me to take better care of myself and to live a more disciplined lifestyle".

Another commented how they had previously been suffering with anxiety, and "piano just makes me want to go on". Consider the impact of playing in terms of actually providing a motivation to live! How much more powerful a benefit could you ask for?

As you can see, there are so many reasons why you may want to play this fantastic instrument, and it can have so many potential benefits for you and your family. But how? How can you actually start putting all this excitement into action, and how many ways do you think there are that you could get up and running? There are actually three ways that most people tend to think of as their choices, and I am going to describe for you the benefits and disadvantages of each. However, there is also a fourth method that does not get talked about as much it should be, and it offers you a huge amount of extra benefits on top. More of that shortly, but first, the three ways you might have thought of.

One to one lessons

Once upon a time, in a land before technology became EVERYTHING, there was only really one way to learn to play piano - you found a teacher that lived near your house. Then, every week, come rain or shine, you went to see them at their house for 30 minutes. You dutifully spent half the lesson showing them what you had been practicing (if your parents made you!) during the week, and they corrected your mistakes and set you a new goal for the following week.

In between lessons, you had to rely on your memory to remember what they had told you was wrong, what they had told you was right, and to remember the new goals themselves. It was a bit of a lottery. If you got stuck on something halfway through the week, you were on your own, unless you were lucky enough that someone else in your house could play too. Otherwise, you had to wait until the next lesson to get help, assuming by the time you got to the next lesson you could still remember what the problem was, and there was no guarantee of that. Like I said, it was a bit of a lottery.

Then there was the fact that unless someone had recommended the teacher as being of good quality, it was likely that you or your parents had never hired a piano teacher before, so there was always the worry as to whether they would be any good, and in fact how would you know if they were not. Of course there was also the question as to whether you and your teacher would get on personality-wise, or whether you would be a good fit musically. What happened if your teacher liked you to figure out problems for yourself, but you responded well to demonstrations that you could copy? What happened if you could have been a great jazz pianist if your teacher was able to nurture your interest, but you ended up being taught by someone who only knew how to teach classical piano? And what happened if having music notation explained to you a different way might have unlocked your understanding but your teacher only knew the way their teacher had taught them?

Did I mention it was a bit of a lottery??

Of course there are some amazing teachers who teach one to one like this, and it would be madness to suggest otherwise. It is just that in order to benefit from them, you have to be prepared to accept a number of things. Firstly, you need to be lucky enough to live near one, or be prepared to travel to where they are. Of course these days, I and many teachers who specialise in one to one teaching can use video conferencing technology to teach you remotely wherever you are in the world, but many other instrumental teachers are still resistant to embracing this alternative fully. You also have to accept that you may not find someone who is perfect for you first time, and be prepared for the potential upheaval of starting with one person and then changing to another. As previously mentioned, it is likely that you will not have any support from your teacher in between lessons at the moment you need it, and of course you will usually need to commit to a regular time slot, working around your teacher's availability.

Group lessons

Over the last 20 to 30 years, group lessons have become a more widely available option for those looking to learn piano. Often run by schools, colleges or community based projects, these can provide a more cost effective way of learning when compared to the individual service of learning one to one. Like learning with a teacher of your own, there is still the need to commit to a regular time slot, almost certainly in some kind of public building, and you are similarly unlikely to have any support in between sessions should you need it when you are stuck on something.

The number of other learners in your group will clearly affect greatly how much attention you can expect to receive from the teacher. It is likely that people will pick up the skills that they are being shown at a range of different speeds, so there is a lot of responsibility on the teacher to make sure that everyone feels like they are getting enough support during a session if they have a problem with something, and likewise are being given enough opportunity to stretch their skills should they pick up something more easily, rather than having to wait for others.

How many other people there are in the classroom will also affect how much money you might be expected to invest in learning this way, with bigger groups allowing institutions to potentially charge less per student, but of course also meaning that you potentially get less individual attention from the teacher. As long as you are prepared for these compromises, group lessons can be a good way for you to 'dip your toe' into the world of learning a new instrument with relatively little financial risk, and see whether it is something you have an interest in longer term. Group sessions are often run over a limited set number of weeks (commonly 6-12 weeks), and so therefore require little in the way of long term commitment, although this may mean that if you do enjoy it enough to want to continue, you are quickly needing to find another solution for when the course ends.

Use an app

Like in many other areas of our lives, the use of technology in learning piano has become increasingly prevalent in recent years. One of the main ways that this has happened with rising popularity is through the use of apps so that people have the flexibility of learning from home at a time that is convenient to them. A huge benefit of this, particularly for adult learners, is this no longer means that they need to be fixed to a regular time or day slot, meaning they can make their hobby fit around their work and family commitments with much more ease.

Another benefit of using an app to learn is they can often involve relatively low cost subscriptions when compared to paying for in person lessons, so represent a low risk way to see if you enjoy your new hobby. Being able to access your content on a range of devices is also a huge benefit, meaning you also have an element of portability in terms of where you do your learning, assuming you also have a portable keyboard. Depending on the app, you may have the ability to manipulate the sound or video of the content you are learning to slow it down to make it easier to copy, and of course having access to recorded content means that you can watch it more than once as and when you need to.

Unfortunately with many apps, you do not have the facility to get any support when you need it. You are paying for access to the tuition content, but it often does not come with any access to a tutor of whom you can ask questions, a facility to get feedback on your playing, or the chance to combat any bad habits you are unknowingly forming.

The other way

There is another way, and it is not as common as it should be.

The potential benefits throughout all of the other ways of learning tend to revolve around how much support from a teacher you can or cannot expect to get access to. Plus for many busy adults, there is the crucial question as to how much flexibility there is with where and when you can learn, and how you can easily you can fit it in to your life.

When I help people to play the music they love inside my online membership, my members have 24/7 access to the huge library of recorded video content from complete beginner courses to advanced song tutorials, meaning that wherever or whenever they want to learn they have complete flexibility. I add new content every month, and they are able to request their favourite songs for me to cover, meaning they feel involved and can help make sure there is always something there they will love to learn.

Most importantly I do not want to make content for my members then leave them to try and figure it out on their own. I want to support them every step of the way. That is why we have a WhatsApp group people can choose to join. In there I am available to answer questions that people post. We have a regular Q&A in the group too. And (and this is the best bit!) members can post informal videos of their playing so that I give them help, and provide feedback and encouragement. I always say to them that I do not need to see their faces or how tidy their house is, just let me see you play, even for a few seconds, and you can take advantage of this powerful feature whenever you want.

No more having to wait until the next week to see your teacher to try and remember what you wanted to ask them. No more using recorded content but not having support when you need it.

There is another way, and I call it Piano Legends. And as I mentioned before, at the end of this book, there is a REALLY special offer to get you playing right now. Flick to the back of the book now – it's OK, I will be here when you get back!

* www.steinway.com/news/features/the-benefits-of-playing-piano [Accessed 21-10-2020]

** www.londonpianoinstitute.co.uk/six-reasons-why-playing-piano-is-healthy [Accessed 23-10-2020]

***www.tandfonline.com/doi/epdf/10.1080/09548963.2022.2058354?needAccess=true [Accessed 14-1-2025]

WHAT DO YOU NEED TO GET STARTED

I mentioned that sometimes it can be the terminology used in keyboard descriptions that become a barrier to getting started for new players, so let me help you by giving you some basic pieces of advice that even someone new to this kind of thing can follow. As you might have gathered by now, my passion and mission is to break down as many barriers as I can to playing piano, and so the last thing I would want to put you off getting started is some jargon! In the first chapter, I told you about the amount of size you might need for your instrument depending on what you are buying, but here I want to focus on what equipment you actually need, depending on whether you go down the piano or keyboard route.

What Should You Sit On?

Starting with the simplest option, if you buy an acoustic piano (whatever size it is from a grand piano to an upright), you will not need any additional equipment other than a piano stool. I realise that you may well have a chair in your house that you think will do the job, and you are not sure why you should need an actual piano stool. However, the relationship between the height of the chair you play from and the height of the keys you play, is one of the most important deciding factors in whether you will experience any discomfort, or even pain, long term in your shoulders and back. Therefore, whatever instrument you purchase, whether acoustic or electric, I would recommend you make a piano stool part of your set up. The majority of piano stools are extremely adjustable in height, and so give you a great deal of control and precision in setting up your playing position. They are often relatively inexpensive and therefore a really worthwhile purchase, and as a bonus they commonly have a small storage space within the seat itself for any music or other materials you want to keep. All things considered, piano stools are a good investment.

What Do The Pedals Do?

If you are researching acoustic pianos, you may well soon notice that there can be some variety in how many foot pedals you see positioned underneath where you will sit, with almost certainly two or three (never more). Before we discuss what these pedals do, it is important to understand that you should never let how many pedals a piano has be a deciding factor in a purchase, because when there are two rather than three, the one that is missing is the one that never gets used!

We will start with the most important pedal, and the one that will see by far the most action - the sustain pedal. This is the pedal that will be the rightmost one regardless of whether you have two or three, and will also be the only pedal you have on the vast majority of electric keyboards too. It is worth saying that learning to use the sustain pedal successfully is a skill of its own. As a result of it involving an extra level of coordination on top of using both hands on the keys, it is not something that you should worry about adding when you first start playing, as it will likely hamper or at least slow down your progress.

This pedal is known as the sustain pedal simply because it sustains the sound produced by any note on the piano or keyboard that is pressed after the pedal has been put down. The sound from these notes will then very gradually fade in volume over a much longer time than it would have done otherwise, stopping completely when the pedal is raised again. The ability to do this is crucial to the vast majority of playing, and whilst the amount it is used can vary a little between styles of music, to all intents and purposes you will be using your sustain pedal constantly when you are ready to learn to coordinate it with the playing your hands are doing. As I mentioned, however, I would not recommend trying to incorporate it straight away, as you will probably find that difficult as a beginner. Saying that, trying pressing it down is not going to break it, so if you want to explore what it does and the effect it has on your sound then feel free - I am a huge fan of encouraging adults who are learning piano to try and have a bit more childlike sense of adventure! Pro tip: keep your heel on the floor when you use it, do not lift your whole leg off the floor.

Next we shall look at the pedal that will be at the leftmost of your pedals on an acoustic piano, regardless of whether you have two or three in total, most commonly referred to as the una corda pedal. To understand the concept of how this works inside a piano, and the effect it has on your sound, you need to understand a little bit about how the sound of a piano is produced. When no pedals are pressed down, the sound of each note that you have available to play on a piano is created by three strings inside the body being hit by a hammer when you press the key. When the una corda pedal is put down, the whole internal action of your piano shifts to the right so that the hammers are no longer exactly lined up with the set of three strings they are usually intended for. As a result, when you press a key, the hammer does not strike all three strings. In older pianos, the action would shift so far the hammer would now only hit one string (thus the name una corda), but it in more modern pianos that tend to on average be slightly smaller, the action does not shift as far, so the hammer will strike two of the three strings. Whether one or two strings are struck, the effect is a small reduction in volume and a slight softening in the tone produced.

Whilst it is useful to know how these things work, in practical terms, the usage of this pedal tends to be something that is for more intermediate and advanced players. Indeed, when demonstrating the effect of the pedal on the sound, some learners can barely perceive the difference, and it is fair to say that depending on the piano, the difference can on occasion be fairly small. Taking all this into consideration, especially as the vast majority of electric keyboards do not even have one, the una corda pedal is not something that I would suggest you allow to cause you any concern.

If you have three pedals on your acoustic piano that just leaves the middle one, which is known as the sostenuto pedal. This is the pedal that causes the most misunderstanding for a lot of people, almost certainly as a result of two contributing factors. Firstly, as previously mentioned, many pianos only have two pedals, and when that is the case it is the sostenuto pedal that is missing. The second part of the confusion stems from the definition of the word sostenuto which means in a sustained manner, and as we have already seen, the righthand pedal is a sustain pedal, so why is there a second pedal that seems to do the same job?

The answer lies in a slight distinction between which notes these two different pedals sustain. The sustain pedal that we have already discussed, sustains any keys that are either being pressed when the pedal goes down AND keys that are pressed after the pedal has been depressed and is still down. However, the sostenuto pedal only sustains notes that are being played as the pedal is put down, and NOT keys played afterwards. As you can see, whilst there is this difference, in practical terms it is quite subtle. I can also tell you that I cannot remember ever being asked to use one in a performance or by a composer in, at the time of writing, 38 years of playing piano. Therefore, I can be very confident in telling you not to worry about having one or not on your piano. After all, if a lot of pianos do not have one, you can be reasonably sure you will not find a lot of songwriters demanding you need to use one!

How Will You Hear Your Sound?

Now let us look at how you are going to hear the sound you are making. If it's an acoustic piano, the answer is obvious - you will hear the sound without any additional equipment. However, if you are buying an electric instrument, there are some variables to be aware of. Some electric keyboards and pianos have speakers built into the body of the instrument. They can appear on the top of the body facing upwards towards the ceiling, or sometimes they can appear underneath the body facing the floor. If they are on top of the body, then they will either be behind the keyboard i.e. they will make the keyboard slightly deeper and come further away from the wall, or they will be either side of the keys and make the keyboard slightly wider in terms of needing slightly more wall space. Your decision with regard to this will have little or no affect on the sound, and is more likely to be decided on personal preference of the aesthetics and / or the space in your home you wish to use.

As with other aspects of buying an electric keyboard, you can imagine that there is a great deal of variety of quality speakers that are used by different manufacturers in different price brackets across the marketplace. Of course in an ideal world, you would want to hear the instrument you are buying in person before purchase, but in the age of online shopping this is not always possible. On this point, I often advise people to do their research (or take the advice of someone more experienced in the field). This can commonly be best done by trying to visit at least one physical store to get a feel for what you like, having already looked online at what price the same instruments can be found for by other suppliers so you have a good idea of the price comparison. Many musical equipment suppliers price match with their competitors, and of course it never hurts to ask. In addition, there are always plenty of sound samples on both the websites of manufacturers as well as elsewhere on the internet such as on YouTube, where manufacturers are increasingly commonly creating demo videos of their products. These can be a great way for you to try and get an idea of the sound of the keyboard you prefer.

If you are purchasing an electric piano that has a wooden body, let me give you one piece of advice that is not often talked about when it comes to how the speakers can affect the quality of your sound, and that is WHERE the speakers are positioned. If the speakers are underneath the keys pointing towards the floor, that can really increase the overall 'weight' of the sound, and increase the lower frequencies. Whether this is an improvement or not may come down to personal preference. However, for what it's worth, in my opinion this always adds an extra sense of reality to the piano sound, as lower frequencies tend to be increased on acoustic pianos the further you go down the keyboard.

There is also another slight variable with regard to what shape the wooden body of the electric piano is. Underneath the keys, above where the pedals are, there is sometimes a slot or a gap in the wooden shape. Depending on the position of the speakers, this can sometimes let some of the sound escape. As a result, if it is possible to get an electric piano with a full back panel with no gap in it, this can add an extra level of weight to the sound again, which is usually my personal preference.

Speaking of personal preference, it is right that we discuss some of the major manufacturers of electric instruments out there so that I can give you the benefit of my many years' experience in buying keyboards and pianos. As you might imagine, buying a keyboard is much like buying a car in terms of which make you end up preferring during your piano journey. Some people may swear that Ford makes the best cars, whereas others are big Skoda fans. By the way that is me. In terms of piano playing, I have always felt that the best electric pianos and keyboards are made by Roland, and as such have bought a good number of their products over the years. That is not to say if you prefer another manufacturer's instrument that one of us is right and one of us is wrong. However, my experience has taught me that Roland have, in my opinion, got one critical element of their sound better than any other manufacturer has ever managed to make it, and that is the low, weighty element of the bottom notes on the piano.

As I mentioned previously, I feel like this is where the finer elements and realism of a piano sound are really defined. Whilst of course it is great for the higher keys to have a nice sense of clarity, in my opinion having a strong, full, weighty lower end of the sound is crucial. I can certainly tell you that this is what I always look for when selecting a piano or keyboard, and it is certainly what makes other people's instruments more enjoyable to play when it is present.

Of course, it is not the case that Roland are the only manufacturer to have a good quality piano sound. Other manufacturers such as Korg, Yamaha, Kurzweil, Kawaii, and others, have made some great instruments over the years. It is also certainly true to say that if you want other features on top of a good piano sound, then you should look across the marketplace. For example Kurzweil always had a good reputation for string sounds, and Korg make some great synth sounds. However if all you want is a good piano sound, then I would start your investigations with Roland and work from there. By the way, in the interest of transparency, I am not officially affiliated with Roland so they are not paying me to say this. However, if they would like to, that would be OK!

It is worth pointing out that some electric keyboards have no speakers in them at all, and these are sometimes referred to as stage pianos, as they are commonly used by professional musicians where they are intended to be plugged into a PA system. In order to hear the sound produced by these instruments you will need a separate speaker, usually otherwise described by manufacturers as a keyboard amplifier. These are usually boxes that are designed for use either in the home or rehearsal spaces, and as such are reasonably small on their own, but obviously take up additional floor space so need to be taken into account when you are working out where you are going to put your new instrument.

If you are purchasing a keyboard amplifier, then you will also need something to connect your keyboard or stage piano to the amplifier itself. The lead or cable that you will require, depending on specific keyboard manufacturers, will most commonly have what is known as a jack plug on both ends. As a result most musicians will refer to this as a jack lead, as the custom is that if the same plug is on both ends of a cable, the cable gets the name of the plug. (In contrast, if there are different plugs on each end we insert the word "to" in between, such as if you had a "mini jack to jack lead"). You may also see the term ¼ inch jack plug, which is the same thing. As a comparison you might think of what you see plugged into an iPod or other phone or mobile device, an 1/8 inch jack plug, otherwise known as a minijack. Depending on how far apart you are going to position your keyboard and keyboard amplifier, typically speaking you may want a jack lead of around one to three metres in length. You might be pleased to know that these are usually reasonably inexpensive, and so it is often worth getting a good quality one, as they will last you for many years if they are only going to be used within your home.

Do you need any other peripherals?

If your keyboard or electric piano does not have a wooden body, then you are going to need a keyboard stand of some description for the instrument to sit on. These are usually also relatively inexpensive items, that can last you for many years. Here are some of the things to watch out for, and some of the variations that you will find on the marketplace.

The most common form of keyboard stand is sometimes referred to as an X-stand. That is because it takes the shape of a metal X that folds flat in on itself when you need to store it or transport it. These X-shaped stands can either be single or double-braced. Depending on the weight of your keyboard or electric piano, I always recommend a double-braced one as these usually give a far more solid support for your instrument, and are commonly only a slightly higher cost than single-braced examples.

Some keyboards are designed to sit on something which you might imagine is being a "U shape" if you were looking at it from above i.e. it has two sides designed to sit underneath the two ends of the keyboard, and a longer part that sits along the length of the keyboard. This shape of stand is less common than the X shape and is usually designed to support a specific model of electric keyboard or piano, available for purchase at the same time.

Depending on whether you are comfortable learning with someone else in the room, or your house, you may also want to consider a set of earphones or headphones for your new electric keyboard or piano. As with many other devices, the choice will come down to whether you want in-ear earphones, or on-ear or over-ear headphones. You will find that the plugs on the end of the headphone cables are the same as with many other devices, i.e. minijack or jack plugs. Double check with your keyboard manufacturer or supplier as to what size socket is on your electric keyboard or piano. In my experience there are many different good manufacturers of earphones and headphones available, so a lot of this choice is down to personal preference. However, over the years I have tended to settle on models made by manufacturers such as Sony and AKG. As a slight note of caution, if you are intending to practice with in-ear earphones long-term, it is worth investing in as good a set as you can afford at the time, because cheap earphones can become a little uncomfortable if used for elongated periods. Using over-ear headphones tends to reduce this issue on average.

One final peripheral that you may need to consider is a music stand. With many acoustic pianos, of course, this is literally part of the body of the piano itself, so you will not need an additional item. With many electric keyboards and pianos, the music stand is something that attaches on to the keyboard body in some way and comes with your keyboard purchase, so again you will not need to purchase anything separately. However, a slight word of caution is that some of these can be quite small and so can struggle to hold large sheet music books, particularly if they are thick. If your instrument sits on an X-stand or similar and this sounds like something you would like some flexibility with, a separate floor stand can be purchased to position behind your keyboard. Usually electric pianos that have full wooden bodies will have something to place your music on built in.

The Most Important Feature To Look For

So far in this equipment section, we have primarily focussed on pieces of peripheral equipment that you may need when you are getting set up, and how to get the best sound out of your instrument. In Chapter 1, we also discussed about the range of numbers of notes available. As a quick recap 88 is best and the same as a real piano, 61 is also common and OK as a starting point but probably not long term, 73 or 76 is unusual and will probably do you just fine, 49 is going to be extremely limiting. What we have not yet discussed, is unquestionably the most important feature to look for if you are buying an electric keyboard or piano, and that is to do with the action of the keys themselves.

You might not be aware of the origin of the word piano and why the instrument has that name; I have certainly told this story many times over the years to people who did not previously know. 'Piano' is short for 'pianoforte' which is the instrument's full name. In Italian 'piano' means soft or quiet, and 'forte' means loud, i.e. the instrument is literally named a 'quiet-loud'! Why would we go to the trouble of naming it in such an unusual way?

The answer lies in what keyboard-based instruments came before the invention of the piano, such as a harpsichord. The mechanism inside a harpsichord involves strings being plucked by little hooks when a key is struck by the performer. Crucially, no matter how hard you hit the keys on a harpsichord, the volume of the sound produced remains the same. However, as we have already discussed when talking about the mechanism of the different pedals on a piano, inside a piano the strings are struck by hammers when a key is pressed by the performer. This method of creating sound DOES allow for a change in volume by changing how hard the key is pressed, which in turn affects how fast the hammer comes down and strikes the strings. In short a piano can play both soft and loud, whereas a harpsichord cannot and so is known as a pianoforte, a soft-loud.

So why is this important when it comes to helping you know what to look for when you are choosing an electric piano or keyboard? That is because this is what is known in keyboard specifications as 'touch sensitive', i.e. the harder you hit the key the louder it sounds, just like on a real piano. It is absolutely critical that any keyboard you purchase is touch sensitive, and sometimes the very cheapest keyboards are not. So what happens if your keyboard is NOT touch sensitive? The answer is that even if you only just catch a key the note will still make its 'normal' sound, as in it will sound properly. You might think that this is a great safety net feature to have, in that even if you do not manage to fully strike a note the keyboard will still make the sound you meant for you. However, what this means is that the instrument is making allowances for you that are extremely detrimental to your technique in the medium to long term. Without touch sensitivity you will never learn to properly control your fingers, and, crucially, develop the necessary strength in your fingers to play expressively with a range of dynamics (volumes).

Saying all of this, the vast majority of keyboards will be touch sensitive, especially if they are full size (i.e. have 88 notes). But if you are just starting out with a smaller instrument whilst you see if your new hobby is going to be something you will enjoy longer term, be careful at the lower cost parts of the marketplace to make sure that you are going to have this functionality. If, when you are looking at an instrument's specification you are not sure, or it is not explicit in its description, just Google the brand and model number with the words "touch sensitive" and see if you can confirm it has this feature. It is also worth saying that if you cannot get any clarification specifically about touch sensitivity, if you DO see mention of anything to do with hammer action, weighted keys or semi-weighted keys, then the instrument will definitely be touch sensitive, as these terms all refer to more sophisticated actions underneath the keys, so will do the job nicely for you.

As you get to be more experienced, you will probably find that you prefer weighted keys as they feel more authentically like a real, acoustic piano. However, when you first begin, do not be surprised if they feel slightly harder work to press down, particularly if you are used to playing an instrument where the keys are not. In some ways, this is similar to when you first begin learning to drive a car and the foot pedals and gear stick in someone else's car feel very different.

Maintenance of your instrument

Clearly any ongoing maintenance that may be required will differ greatly depending on whether you have purchased an acoustic piano or electric instrument. I touched upon the subject of the need to regularly tune acoustic pianos in Chapter 1, but it is worth restating in order to make sure your piano is well looked after, because if you do it will potentially last you for a lifetime! On average, depending on how heavily or frequently a piano is used, it is sensible to get it checked by a piano tuner about once a year or so. You can leave them longer than this, but it is best not to go longer than eighteen months to two years, as it is the kind of thing where putting it off can cause larger problems than you would otherwise have had - just like a car!

The main purpose of having a specialist check your piano regularly is to tune the strings inside to make sure they are maintaining their correct pitch. As mentioned earlier, there are multiple strings for every key on the piano, so that is hundreds of strings that can lose tension and become out of tune. However, inside a piano there are many other components (just Google what the inside of a piano looks like if you've never seen one before!) that need to be regularly checked, such as the hammer action itself, and the felts used on the hammers and the damper. Assuming you make sure your piano is looked after, these additional components should only need occasional repair, but they are worth keeping on top of when the need arises to save larger costs long term. In terms of the cost of a piano tuner, at the time of writing here in the north of England, this will typically be around £60-£100. Considering the skill involved and specialist knowledge needed, this is a very worthwhile and relatively minor investment.

If, on the other hand, you purchase an electric keyboard or piano, you will be pleased to know that obviously these do not need regular tuning, so you will not need to take into account those regular costs. However, of course, electric instruments do suffer from equivalent issues from time to time, and whilst acoustic pianos are designed to be relatively straightforward to open up and look inside to find the problem, this can be a more difficult procedure with some electric keyboards. One of the most common issues that electric keyboards can run into is the contacts underneath the keys that transmit the information as to how hard the key has been pressed etc. Over time and with use, these can crack and start to send faulty information. The most frequent sign that this is happening is that keys will randomly suddenly be extremely loud compared to the other notes that you are pressing, or alternatively there will be a fractional delay between you pressing the key and there being any sound at all. When this happens it is unavoidable that you will either need to get your instrument repaired, or you will need to accept the need for a new one, as these issues will only deteriorate over time. The good news is that the cost of the parts to repair this issue is usually extremely cheap (even less than a £1 per key the last time I needed to enquire). However, the cost of the labour can soon mount up as a result of the specialist skill involved. As a result, depending on the age and value of your instrument, sometimes when this happens it can be worth cutting your losses and looking for a new instrument. All things considered, whilst with electric instruments you do not need to worry about the cost of regularly maintaining it like you do with an acoustic piano, it is worth bearing in mind the need for a small 'rainy day' fund for your electric keyboard or piano should it need a repair or replacement.

Summary

I realise that at first glance this may appear to be a lot of separate pieces of equipment that you are going to need or at least consider, and you may be concerned that this is going to be an expensive set up. However, as I explained in Chapter 1, it is not necessary to spend thousands of pounds, particularly at first when you are still deciding whether this is going to be something that you are going to enjoy long-term in your life. Commonly you will find that there are bundles available by some manufacturers, where you will get most (if not all) of the peripheral pieces that you are going to need along with your electric keyboard. At the time of writing it is certainly possible to pick up a beginner bundle for somewhere in the region of £250-£300. Obviously for some people this may be a sum of money that you need to save for over a period of time. However, hopefully you can see that this is not an unachievable fortune that is too out of reach, even with a little saving. And of course, you now know that it is possible to get a lifetime of enjoyment out of playing so I hope that you feel that this is an investment worth making. If I can be of any assistance in helping you choose your equipment, feel free to reach out and I will be happy to help.

You can email me directly at hello@markdeeksmusic.com. I personally reply to every single one.

LET'S GET YOU PLAYING PIANO

I love that you are excited. You have got this far, you are ready to start playing, and of course one of the great things about piano is that you cannot really break anything by just hitting any notes and seeing what sounds come out. So if you want to start putting your fingers on any key you like and seeing what happens, you can absolutely be my guest. Having a childlike sense of adventure when it comes to piano is a great tool to have at your disposal, so keep that in mind. However, whilst you can be encouraged that in some ways you can not really go wrong, let me give you some useful pointers that will at least set you on the right path. Whilst it may not be the most glamorous or rock and roll element of learning to play piano, a good posture and positioning yourself correctly in relation to your instrument is a really important fundamental to try and get right from the beginning, especially in the name of avoiding back, neck and shoulder issues later on.

Finding your way around and which note is which?

First of all, let us get you sat positioned correctly horizontally (left to right) in relation to the keys. You may have heard of the note "middle C". As your keyboard could have anything from 49 to 88 notes you can be forgiven for thinking that this might be a harder process than it is. In basic terms, the musical alphabet only involves seven lettered notes from A to G, and as far as a piano or keyboard is concerned, they move from left to right across the keyboard, and then the pattern begins again. Do not expect that the lowest note, therefore, will always be an A. Commonly on an acoustic piano this IS the case, but most commonly on electric keyboards (unless full size) it is not. Likewise, the highest note across the board is almost always a C. I did not promise you it would always be logical!

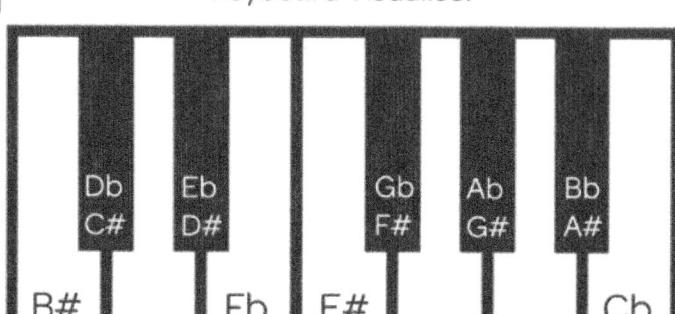

Keyboard Visualiser

As you can see on the Keyboard Visualiser, as well as seven different shaped white notes on a piano, there are also five different black notes before the pattern begins again. You can also see that the five black notes are grouped in a pair and a three. The seven white notes are the seven letters of the musical alphabet, A to G, however this is a moment that I need to make some critical points that I believe are often not stressed sufficiently, and lead to repeated misunderstandings for a lot of beginners.

Firstly, please remember that white and black notes are a 'piano concept' not a 'music concept', i.e. this is a distinction only relevant to piano players. I have encountered countless people learning the piano who seem to have got the impression that black notes are somehow 'different' in some way. I always say the same thing: "No, they're just further away!" I think part of this misunderstanding is down to the fact that most piano players will be taught to play their first exercises only involving white notes, and so psychologically there is already a barrier drawn between the first notes that they learn and those strange looking black notes. I understand why people do it, and as you will soon see, I do it too because it is certainly easier to get someone to play their first patterns using the keys that are nearest to them. But please do not think there is any more difference between the white and black notes than that. There are only 12 different notes, but those 5 black notes are not 'harder' notes, it just so happens that they are slightly further away from you.

Secondly, as you can see in the Visualiser, every note in music has more than one name. Sorry, I'm just the messenger boy! Rather than panic about how complicated you think this is going to make things, let me reassure you by helping you to compare it to how languages work. If we want to write the "ay" sound in the English language as in the word "day", we spell it "ay". However, we can also get the same sound in the word "straight" by using the letters "aigh". The French, on the other hand, can use "é" in the word "café" and get the same effect. So in this particular instance, there are three ways of getting the same sound, and each is written down differently. Music works in a similar way. For example, an F# (F sharp) and a Gb (G flat) are two different names for the same sounding note, and we will use one name or the other depending on which musical key we are in. When you hear musicians use the word "key" in this way, replace it with the word "language" and this will help you to understand the kind of comparisons that we can draw between words and musical notation.

To sharpen a note means to go one note higher (on a piano one note to the right), and to flatten a note means to go one note lower (on a piano this is one note to the left). The best way that I can give you to remember this is to think about how if you climbed up a mountain you would reach a sharp point at the top, and if you climbed back down again you would arrive at a flat field. Therefore, sharp is up and flat is down! Crucially (and this is a mistake that SO many beginners make), this does NOT mean that the note that you land on when you sharpen or flatten a note will definitely be a black note. In the previous example, sharpening an F makes an F# (a black note), and flattening a G makes a Gb (the same black note).

However, if you look at the next image you will see that there are two places on a keyboard where this is not the case, as there are no black notes between a B and a C, and an E and an F (indicated by the circles). But do not make the mistake of thinking that there are no B sharps (the same note as C), C flats (B), E sharps (F) or F flats (E) - there are all of those! Check back to the Keyboard Visualiser if you don't believe me!

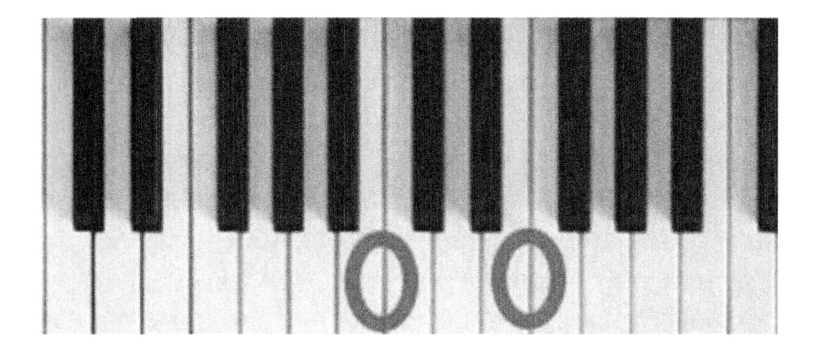

Before you start thinking that this is all too complicated, I would heartily recommend that at this stage you do not worry too much about this. The important concepts to grasp right now are that there are a total of twelve different notes in music, each can have more than one name depending on which musical language (key) we are talking in, and it just so happens that on a piano seven of the notes are white and five are black, remembering that black notes are not 'different' nor do they equal sharp or flat. They are just further away!

How should you sit and what height should things be?

As I previously mentioned, this is an important subject to make sure you do not have issues with back, shoulder and neck pain as you start to sit at the keyboard for longer periods of time. You should sit with both of your feet flat on the floor. When you are ready to start using a pedal, you should rest the ball of your foot on the pedal and leave your heel on the floor at all times - you are not pumping up a car tyre!

If you are playing an acoustic piano or an electric piano with a wooden body, you are not going to have much flexibility in terms of the height of the keys in relation to you. In these circumstances the height and angle of what you sit on becomes even more critical, as you are in control of this. Many people try to use a dining chair or something similar, but of course dining chairs are usually not adjustable in terms of their height. As a result, they are not always the best option for playing piano. When looking for a piano or keyboard you will often see specialist piano stools available for sale and be tempted to discount them as an unnecessary additional cost, especially considering you already have chairs at home. However, the major advantage piano stools have is that they are height adjustable, as well as often including a small storage space, which can be really useful for your sheet music and anything else that you might need whilst playing the piano.

Another advantage of piano stools is it they are often completely flat on the top surface, unlike some dining chairs. By having a flat surface to sit on this should improve your posture and mean that you do not end up hunched or sat at an awkward angle when trying to reach the keyboard which of course itself is flat. As I previously mentioned, if you have a piano (be it acoustic or electric) with a wooden body, then you have no height adjustment possibilities with your instrument itself, therefore a piano stool is a great option to make sure that you do not have incorrect posture. They are not usually very expensive and so can be a great investment that will last you for many years, and provide great flexibility in terms of height adjustment.

As I mentioned in Chapter 3 about the equipment you need to get started, if you have an electric keyboard or similar it is going to be sat on a keyboard stand of some description. With these you have way more options in terms of height adjustment to make sure that your posture is correct. This is because keyboard stands will usually have a number of height adjustment settings available. On the most common X-shaped keyboard stands, you will commonly see two different forms of height adjustment, situated at the centre of the X, usually on some kind of disc. The first will be a series of what are sometimes referred to as "alligator teeth" on the central disc, where you will have a handle to clamp the teeth in place in your chosen position. This type of stand usually allows for a good range of height adjustment with small incremental changes between each position. The second type is a series of holes around the disc in the centre of the stand, with some sort of small bolt that you can put through your chosen hole. These sometimes allow for less flexibility in height adjustment as there will be gaps between each hole, and you may have to make a compromise when choosing a perfect height. As a result I tend to prefer the ones with teeth as the differences between each height setting are usually more gradual.

Whatever combination of items you have, and whatever options you have in terms of relative height, you are trying to get the keys that you are playing to come over the top of your knees, as well as trying to make sure that your pelvis and back positions mean that you are sitting up straight. It can be very easy to get into a habit of slouching when you play (and take it from me it is a VERY hard habit to break!). You should avoid having the keyboard at a height that means that you have to hunch your shoulders in relation to the height of your forearms coming away from your body. To check this position, I often tell people to pretend they are a young child who is pretending to be a zombie. By that I mean relax your arms by the side, then raise your forearms to an approximately 90° angle, and for the full effect (the optional extra!), make a sound like a zombie or ghost! You want this to feel like as natural position as possible so that your shoulders are not hunched. Neither should you feel like you are having to reach down to reach the keyboard, because if the keys are too low you may also end up with a painful back, shoulder and neck. Whilst any issues may not be immediately apparent, this is a part of your set up that is worth monitoring over a period of time. If at any stage you start to experience any pain, stiffness, or discomfort, it is worth considering all of the height options that you have available to you to see if even a slight change may make some difference.

Moving around the keyboard

For the vast majority of your playing, your arms will stay very close to your sides and your elbows should not point away from you as you move around the keyboard. As my piano teacher used to say to me when I was a child, you are not a chicken flapping its wings! It is also extremely important that you do not twist your wrist if you need to reach combinations of notes. This is especially the case when you are playing combinations of white and black notes where the black notes (remember they are slightly further away!) are to be played by a shorter finger such as your little finger or thumb. It can be tempting for a beginner to use the small amount of sideways movement that you have in your wrist to help with this, but this is extremely bad technique, and will quickly cause stiffness or even pain in your wrist. Instead, keep your wrists and forearms in as much of a straight line as much as possible. Then, simply move your fingers higher up the keys (slightly further away from you) until the combination of notes that you need are within reach.

When you first start trying to use this method, you will almost certainly need to make conscious decisions to move up the keys when you feel you need to. However, as your skills develop, you should look to be able to employ a more advanced version of the technique. Rather than only adjusting your hand to a new position horizontally as notes arrive that call for it, you can also slide up the keys (and back down again) at the same time as keys are pressed down. Ideally you will learn to do this in advance of when you are going to be need to be there. As I say, this is a more advanced technique, so do not expect to be able to master that quickly (as aside from anything else it means needing to be able to look ahead in the music to see what is coming). However, it is a great concept to familiarise yourself with even in the beginning. Therefore I would encourage you to press some random notes down and whilst they are down get used to what it feels like to slide up or back down the keys, and notice how much more flexibility it gives you in your manoeuvrability around the keyboard.

Learning how to control your fingers

Before we get to actually playing some notes, all I want you to do is now start looking at your hand. You might never have noticed this before, but if you try to move any of your fingers individually, at least one other finger will also move slightly. The fingers are interconnected by muscles inside your hand, and this means that it is literally impossible to only move one finger in isolation. So what is the impact of this for a piano player? Obviously we need to be able to only play one note at once, and we certainly do not want other notes going down at the same time if we do not want them to.

Of course the trick is being able to control our finger movement sufficiently to make sure that we only play the notes that we need. So is there a way that you can practice this without actually having a keyboard in front of you? Obviously ideally you want to be making a sound, as that is when the fun starts. However it will not always be possible to be sat at your keyboard, and there maybe parts of the day when you have five minutes to yourself that you could still be practising something useful. The good news is that even when are you waiting for someone, in a meeting, sat at the bus stop, watching the TV, or whatever it is, you can still be doing something to improve your piano playing technique.

What I want you to try right now is to curve the fingers of your hand slightly as if you have a small ball in it, perhaps a tennis ball. Then, keeping your hand in that shape, I want you to turn your hand over so that you are looking at the back of your hand. Then, again keeping this shape, I want you to hold your hand just above the top of a surface, such as a table, your knee, or whatever else there is to hand. Ideally you should be sat in the kind of position I described before, sat up straight with your arms by your side, in a similar way to how you might sit at a computer keyboard. Crucially, I do not want your fingertips to be touching the surface, they must be hovering just above it. Then, all I want you to do is to try and touch the surface with one finger at a time, starting with your thumb and moving through your hand until you use your little finger, then come back down to the thumb. Remember, you are not starting with your fingertips touching the surface and lifting the fingers one by one, you are starting with your fingertips just above the surface and touching the surface one by one.

Now I want you to realise that as you do so, this is probably unlike any other physical movement that you have ever done in your life. The one similarity that can be drawn is with people who are able to touch type on a computer keyboard. Of course most of us who type or use a computer regularly probably rely on our stronger fingers. By that I mean probably mostly use our thumbs, index fingers, and middle fingers. It is a more advanced typing ability to be able to also use our ring fingers and little fingers independently with the same kind of accuracy and consistency. To do so is a skill that is usually taught to people who are learning to touch type at great speed.

Not just in relation to typing, but most of us do not use our ring or little fingers independently for anything at all. Think about it. Almost every task that you use your hands for, involves your fingers working as a team. This could be anything from picking up a pen to pointing, pushing, throwing, or whatever skills that you use your fingers for on a day to day basis. Remember the first time that you learned to tie a tie, or to tie your shoe lace? Even this kind of complex task involves using your fingers together. We so rarely use fingers independently of each other, especially not assigning equal responsibility for all of our fingers on both hands. The first time you sit down and try and play piano you will be quickly aware of this challenge. However, the good news is that this is the same for absolutely everyone. So when you first find this difficult, I want you to cling on to that, remember it, and above all do not worry. This is just part of the process, and it is my mission to make sure that you are doing things correctly and are ready to play.

When you first start getting used to this feeling, I want you to keep doing that exercise for a few minutes at a time every chance you get, at least once or twice a day. As with many things when you are learning piano, little and often is the key to your success. Try to make sure that at any one moment you are not letting the fingers that are NOT touching the surface start to point forwards away from you, or worse, towards the ceiling. All of your fingers, at all times, should remain in that lightly curved shape with the finger tips just fractionally above the surface. At first you may feel like you need to get the fingers not in use 'out of the way', and you might also feel like they suddenly have a mind of their own, but you will soon learn to control them and make them do what you want. Just do not be surprised if that is more difficult than it sounds at first!

Also, please do not make the mistake of only doing this with your right hand, or left hand if you are left-handed. Obviously, you realise that you are going to need to be able to develop these skills and finger control equally in both hands if you are going to be able to play the piano, so making sure that you spend sufficient time practising this with both hands is essential.

Now here comes one of the best pieces of advice I can give you as you start your journey to being able to play the piano. Right from the beginning, even this very first exercise, even if you are not sat at a keyboard, once you think you can do an exercise, I want you to try and do it without looking at your hands. Being able to play without looking at your hands is often seen as a much more advanced skill, that surely cannot be accessible to people who are just beginning, and of course in many ways this is true. But, and I think this is a huge big critical but, I believe it is so important that even beginners learn to feel what it feels like to move their fingers independently, without feeling that they have to see it with their eyes in order for it to happen successfully. It really is the case that your brain is capable of doing way more than you believe, and too much reliance on hand eye coordination will be a huge barrier to you being able to play the piano successfully.

In addition I am a huge believer in the importance of protecting your confidence, and the psychological and motivational aspects of learning to play an instrument. It can be a lonely business at times, filled with many possible potholes on the way. This is one of the reasons that the That Piano Guy Club community aspect of what I do is so important. Not only am I able to answer questions directly and provide feedback on videos that people post of their playing, but the community is able to support each other in a way that no one to one lesson can replicate. Knowing that there are lots of other players just like you at a similar stage to you, to support and cheerlead or keep you accountable is a huge psychological boost.

As I feel really strongly that it is important to protect your motivation and enjoyment as you go, I want you to remember what it was like when you were young, and another child said to you that they could do something without looking at it. It sounded like they had mastered it, that they were better than you, and it gave them huge confidence. That kind of confidence is priceless when you are learning how to play an instrument. So right from the beginning, with every single thing that you attempt to do, once you have had a few goes at it and think that you are making a little bit of progress, try and do it without looking. This can mean that you either close your eyes, look out of the window, or at anything else just as long as it is something other than your hands. Most importantly make sure that your head is up so that you are not crouched over the keyboard, even if your eyes are closed. We want you to get used to the feeling of your head being up, because that is how you are going to be able to look at music or perform to an audience. If you allow yourself to get used to being crouched over the keys, and particularly if you feel you need to see something in order for it to happen, then I promise you that this is one of the hardest habits to break if we let it go on for too long. It is simply impossible, even with peripheral vision, to see everything that you are going to need when you are playing the piano fluently. Therefore you have to get used to that fact, work on convincing your brain, start to believe, and get confidence from the fact that you are capable of doing things without seeing them.

Oh and there is one more reason to really see if you can work on developing this skill: I can practically guarantee you that you will perform better without seeing your hands than with. I am not suggesting that it will be perfect especially at first, of course not. But by making yourself not look at your hand, what you are doing is you are removing an element of too much information from your brain. You know how when you are looking for something on a shelf and it is right in front of you, but you do not see it? You will say you looked at it but did not SEE it. That is exactly the same as what is happening when you are seeing your hands playing piano for the first time. Your brain is not processing everything that your eyes are seeing, because you are not used to what you are seeing yet: there is too much information. As an experienced piano player of many years, I am able to glance at my hands and quickly assess the situation, almost without thought. However, when you are first beginning playing you are not yet able to do this. Rather than see this as a hindrance or a problem, what I want you to do is take it as an opportunity to allow your brain to get used to the feel of playing the instrument, because you are going to rely on feel when you are playing the keyboard far more than you could possibly imagine.

In winter 2017, I was performing in Austria at an outdoor Christmas market. By this time I had been playing the piano for 35 years, and for most of that time I had been playing professionally. I had performed hundreds and hundreds, if not thousands of times in front of audiences of all sizes, in all kinds of locations. It was certainly not the first time that I had performed outdoors, but it was certainly one of the coldest. Despite the fact that I was performing music that I had performed many times before, within minutes of starting the performance I quickly realised just how cold it was and what kind of impact this was going to have on my fingers.

As I have commonly done in the past for outdoor performances, I was wearing fingerless gloves to try and strike a balance between keeping my hands as warm as possible, but also being able to feel the keys when I perform. However, despite having had fully fingered gloves on till the last moment before it was time to play, within only a few minutes of beginning the performance the tips of my fingers started to go ever so slightly numb. I did not lose feeling totally, because of course my fingers were very active at this moment. However, I was suddenly very conscious that even with a slight loss of feel, playing piano became much more difficult than it would be normally, even for someone who has been playing for many years. Whilst I was able to call upon my professional experience to cope with the situation, I certainly remember needing to concentrate just a little bit harder than normal in order to make sure of what I was doing. Many people suggested that I should perform with fingered gloves, but I know that the feeling of my skin on the keys is too important to do that. So, let that be a lesson next time you are performing at a Christmas market in Austria: wear fingerless gloves but keep your fingers moving!

Which finger is which? Your first exercises - you can not go wrong!

One of the things that can commonly put adults off getting started playing piano, is that they might have tried before but been faced with boring, child-like books that make them learn how to play nursery rhymes. Nothing demotivates a busy adult who wants to play music by their favourite artist faster than being asked to play Frère Jacques or Old MacDonald! Not on my watch. Sure, at first you are going to need to play a few patterns and exercises to get your fingers used to playing the keys independently, but once you have a few under your belt, you will feel equipped to start playing the songs you love, and I will have shown you some tricks that will make them sound like music not exercises as fast as possible.

On both hands your thumb is called number one. Just take a moment to realise what that means as obviously your hands face the opposite way to each other. The critical thing to realise for beginners is that your fingers are NOT numbered left to right, they are numbered from thumb to little finger on both hands, so your thumb is number one all the way through to your little finger being number five. Therefore, a great thing for you to do right from your first exercises is to think to yourself, or even better say out loud, which finger number you are pressing at any one moment. At this stage you might not even be playing an actual piano or keyboard yet, you may just be tapping the table but that is fine.

Remember, if you can do this without looking in your hands and therefore concentrate on getting used to how it feels, it will serve you well in the long run.

Whilst it is great to be able to do the first exercises I described above without a keyboard in front of you, of course the fun starts when you actually start playing some notes. At this stage I would like to take a minute to encourage you that it really does not matter which notes you start playing these first patterns on. Do not worry about right or wrong notes right now, you can not break it by playing some notes rather than others. As I have previously mentioned, having a childlike sense of adventure and employing a "what does this button do?" approach when it comes to just playing notes can be really beneficial. Just put your hands on some notes and start playing, and if you find a sound or a combination of sounds that you like the sound of, take a photo of it on your phone or record a short video of it, and keep these somewhere. You never know when you may want to refer to them sometime, and if nothing else they will act as a great document of your progress as you go.

Saying all of that, whilst as this is not a music theory book we do not need to worry about why, most piano players will start working on their first patterns by putting their right hand thumb (and left hand little finger) on a C, and then lying each subsequent finger on the next white note to the right (going up the keyboard). In doing this, your fingers in each hand will be over a C, D, E, F and G.

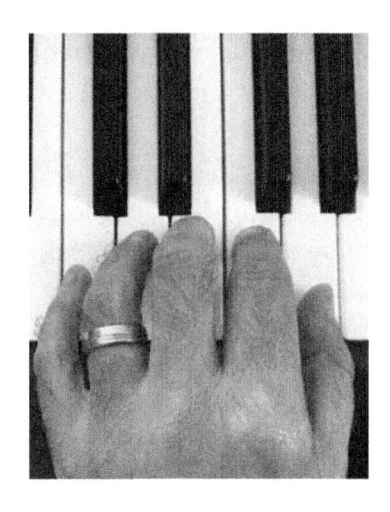

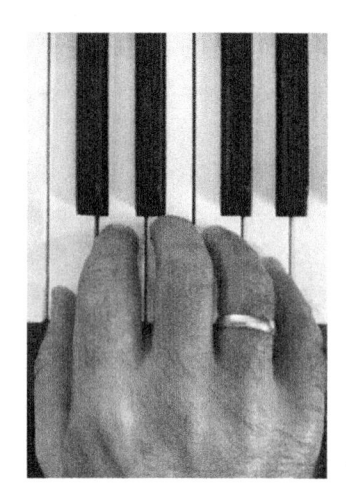

Rest each finger on, or as close as possible to on, each key, and press them down in turn from left to right then back down to where you started, and do this for both the right and left hand, separately for now. In terms of piano fingering you have just played:

Exercise 1:
Right Hand
    1   2   3   4   5   4   3   2   1

Equivalent Notes for the Left Hand
    5   4   3   2   1   2   3   4   5

Make sure that your wrists are roughly in line with the top of the white keys. i.e. pretend there is a piece of paper lying on the white keys, and your wrist should touch that piece of paper as it comes off the keyboard. If you lift your wrists too high it becomes very difficult to see what is going on in your hands. If you let it drop below that imaginary line, it starts to become increasingly difficult to move your fingers. Remember that the fingers that are not being used at any one time should try not to leave contact with the keys, and should certainly not be pointing upwards towards the ceiling. Keep all fingers over all the keys at all times. Do not worry if this is tricky at first, with little and often practice this will gradually improve.

Of course, whilst this is an obvious pattern to begin with, most tunes do not have melodies that run in such sequential order, so it is a good idea to get started with some more 'jumbled up' patterns. Here come some of the exercises that I always recommend to begin with. They are listed with the fingering for the right hand first, and you will see that I have also listed the equivalent exercise for the left hand each time as well (i.e. to end up with the same notes in each hand, the finger numbers need to be reversed). For example, if you are playing alternate notes in the right hand with number 1, in order to get the same notes in the left hand you would play alternate notes with number 5.

Exercise 2:

Right Hand
1 2 1 3 1 4 1 5

Equivalent Notes for the Left Hand
5 4 5 3 5 2 5 1

Exercise 3:

Right Hand
5 1 5 2 5 3 5 4

Equivalent Notes for the Left Hand
1 5 1 4 1 3 1 2

Exercise 4:

Right Hand
    4   1   4   2   4   3   4   5

Equivalent Notes for the Left Hand
    2   5   2   4   2   3   2   1

Exercise 5:

Right Hand
    1   3   2   4   3   5   2   4

Equivalent Notes for the Left Hand
    5   3   4   2   3   1   4   2

Whilst these are a good selection to use at first, in reality it almost does not matter which pattern of fingers you practice, as long as all of your fingers are being worked independently. It is of course true that your ring and little fingers are physically weaker than the others, so it is worth making sure that they get some special attention, but just make sure that all your fingers are getting a workout and you will be fine. Likewise, as I mentioned earlier, whilst we commonly use the notes starting on a C for most basic piano exercises, it really does not matter where you put your hands, just at this stage try and have the same notes in both hands (although to be honest even THAT does not really matter!). What I want to do is make sure that you consciously protect your sense of enjoyment and motivation. If you start to get sick of the sound of trying these exercises in one place on the keyboard, move to some different notes immediately! And if you find some combinations that you like, as I said before, make a note, take a photo or make a video. These tips will all help to make sure you enjoy yourself.

Remember, this is going to feel REALLY weird at first! Your fingers are not used to working independently of each other, especially those weaker ones, ESPECIALLY the weaker ones on your weaker hand. So do not worry if this is the case, it is this way for everyone. Saying that, here are three things to watch out for to try and make sure you are avoiding, as these can turn into bad habits if we are not careful.

First, because your ring and little fingers are comparatively weak, it is not uncommon for people to start tilting their hands slightly on a diagonal horizontally towards those fingers, i.e. their stronger fingers start to come further away from the keys. It is almost as if your hand is starting to try and lean in to give extra backup to the weak fingers. Try to make sure that your hands stay straight horizontally so that you can see the backs of your hands equally across, and that it is your fingers doing the work, not your hand starting to help out.

Next, as I previously mentioned, you need to try and make sure that your wrists stay roughly in line with an imaginary line coming off the top of the white keys. When you first begin playing, this may feel like an unnatural position to hold, or at least maintain for very long, and so a very common issue for beginners is for their wrists to start to slouch below this height. When this happens I believe that it is a subconscious reaction to your fingers not feeling strong enough to do what they are being asked to do, and your brain trying to lend some extra weight to the movement from your palm and wrist. Whilst I do not expect that you will be able to stop this happening entirely, at least be aware of the possibility of it and try and correct it as soon as possible when it does.

The last of the things to watch out for here is to keep an eye on your forearms and see if your arms are moving up and down as you play each key. If they are, stop! In exactly the same way as I have described above with your hands and wrists wanting to help out, this is just your arms attempting to do the same. The best way to think of all this is to think about what would happen if you tried to open a push door with just one finger. In all likelihood, you would find that an individual finger would not be strong enough to open a door on its own. So, without thinking, you would start adding more fingers, or your full hand, followed by your wrist digging in, then your arm, and (if necessary) your shoulder and body. In short, we are hardwired to start adding extra strength all the way from the tip of a finger to your body if we try to push something and we are not able. What is more, is that this all usually happens in a split second without us consciously thinking about it. As a result, when it comes to playing the piano and our fingers feeling weak when needing to press things, our brain goes into autopilot and tries to help out. The problem is that piano playing needs to come from the fingers. As you might imagine, whilst you could theoretically have time to move your arms up and down for every note for your first slow notes, when you have more advanced skills and are playing much faster music, not only would you not have time for that, that would be a lot of wasted effort and energy.

What comes next?

Obviously there comes a time when you need to move from playing one note at once to two notes and more. It is worth saying that the exercise that I am about to recommend is one that many piano teachers would wait quite a while before suggesting you try, as for many people first starting out this is quite a bit harder. However, I think that in this instance, you are going to have to try this eventually so why not dive in, have a go, and find out what you are up against. I mean find out what fun lies in store! As I say, though, this is quite a step up from the single note exercises, so do not panic if it takes a while for you to be able to successfully do the next exercise.

One of the previous patterns was:

Right Hand
  1   3   2   4   3   5   2   4

Equivalent Notes for the Left Hand
  5   3   4   2   3   1   4   2

Now instead of playing those notes individually, I want you to try and combine each pair of notes and play them at the same time rather than one after another. Again feel free to put them anywhere you like on the piano, but most commonly piano players again tend to start this on the notes C to G.

Exercise 6:

Right Hand
  1&3   2&4   3&5   2&4

Equivalent Notes for the Left Hand
  5&3   4&2   3&1   4&2

When you try this pattern it is likely that whatever fingers are not being used at any given moment will do one of two things, almost whether you like it or not! Firstly you may find that you want to try and get the non-playing fingers out of the way to such an extent that they start lifting quite a way from the keys, even to the point of almost pointing upwards. Do not worry, this is very common, but remember that you need to try and avoid that wherever possible. It is important that even now when you are playing two notes at once, you try and keep the other fingers nice and close to the keys as that is the position you will need them in when it comes to wanting to play with increased speed. Any distance for them to have to travel to play is wasted energy and, of course, takes time, no matter how small a time that is. A very small distance from the keys when you first start trying to do this is not a problem, as long as they are not pointing upwards. You will find as you practice this more that your non-playing fingers become easier to control.

The alternative, almost opposite issue you may have when you try this exercise is that you struggle to get your non-playing fingers out of the way at all and you find yourself playing extra notes as well as the two you want at any moment. Again, do not panic, this is a very common problem at first, but it is something that you will need to practice avoiding as your skills develop. As with all of your first attempts at playing, little and often is the secret. A few minutes here, a few minutes there of each different pattern, and you will soon find that things start to improve. Remember, trying to sit for a long period of time doing the same thing over and over again is very much counter-productive, especially when you are first playing. Just because you are an adult does not mean you are ready to go straight to playing for an hour: these are new skills and, in many cases, new physical movements that take some getting used to. Again, when you think you have managed to play a few notes successfully, try and play them again without looking at your hand. Continually try and build your confidence in this way and you will reap the rewards later.

Here comes your real game changer (part 1)

So far everything we have done has involved your hands covering a five-note range on the piano, regardless of which pattern you were playing or where you decided to put your hands. But of course not everything on the piano fits within five note ranges, so it is time to show you the pianist's hand move that is one of the most important things that you will learn at any stage. When you learn this it is a real game changer, and if that sounds dramatic that is because it is. In fact I often refer to this as the pianist's sleight of hand, as eventually you will be doing this so quickly without even thinking about it. For now, though, let us take this one stage at a time. If you want to see me demonstrate this, watch the video at http://bit.ly/pianosleightofhand, and give my YouTube channel a Subscribe whilst you are there!

You have probably never thought about the significance of your thumb effectively being sideways to the rest of your hand before. Obviously this 'feature' helps us to grip and hold things in our hands in everyday life. However, it is actually hugely significant in piano playing too. So much so that when you realise what this allows you to do on a keyboard, you should feel pretty excited! I want you to turn your right hand over so that you are looking at your palm. Then I want you to take your thumb and touch the bottom of your index finger with it. Then do the same with your middle finger and fourth (ring) finger, then do the same process with your other hand. Hopefully this should be fairly easy for you to do.

Now turn your right hand back over so that you can see the back of your hand and your fingers are back over the keys. As before, put your thumb over a C, and each finger over the subsequent notes up to G. Now play the first three notes, C to E, and pause whilst you are holding the E down. I want you to notice that with that 3rd finger pressing a note, and your fingers slightly curved, there is effectively a tunnel created under your fingers. If you need a better view of what I mean, physically lean to the side temporarily and look underneath your hand (or see me do it at http://bit.ly/pianosleightofhand). Still with your 3rd finger holding down the E I want you to move your thumb 'through the tunnel' and see if you can touch the bottom of your 4th finger. If you cannot quite reach far enough do not worry, but see how close you can get. If you need to remind yourself of the movement you are using, go back to the earlier stage before you played the notes where you had your palm facing you and you touched the base of each finger with your thumb. It is the same movement.

Why is this such a big deal for a piano player? Well, put your fingers back on the keys and I will show you. Again, play the first three notes from C to E, and get to the stage where your 3rd finger is holding down the E. The next you are going to play is the F next to it, but rather than using your 4th finger which is over it, you are going to use your thumb again, i.e. you will have played C, D, E and F, with fingers 1, 2, 3 and 1. Then you will be able to use the rest of your fingers to play a G (2nd finger), A (3rd finger), B (4th finger) and finally C (5th finger). In total you have played eight different notes, so this one small move has broken you out of that five-note range you were restricted by before. At first getting to the F with your thumb might feel like it is physically a long way away, even though you can see that it is in reality a very small distance. You may well find that you have an overwhelming temptation as you do it to turn your hand slightly anticlockwise whilst your 3rd finger is holding the E in order to 'lift' your hand out of the way. If this is you right now, you must resist, and here is why.

Firstly, we know that you do not actually NEED to. We have already proven that you can reach the base of your 4th finger with your thumb without twisting your hand, and just because you are holding a note down with your 3rd finger, nothing about that has changed. Secondly, if you DO make the mistake of twisting your hand anticlockwise, you will find that causes your elbow to leave your side. That is a wholly unnecessary movement and, as I think you will have realised by now, I am all about trying to minimise and streamline your movements as you learn to manoeuvre around the keyboard, because the more you pay attention to that at this stage, the faster you will be able to play in the long run. As I have already mentioned, when I was learning as a young child my piano teacher taught me that if let my arms leave my side as I did this I would end up looking like a chicken flapping its wings from behind, especially if I did it with both hands, and I have never forgotten that!

So what is the trick to pulling off this manoeuvre WITHOUT twisting your hand? Simple - just keep reminding yourself that when you were not touching the keys you had no difficulty in touching the base of the different fingers with your thumb. What you are looking for as you do this move is for the back of your hand to stay flat and in a straight line with the rest of your arm as much as possible. In addition, you want the whole process of moving your five fingers to a different part of the piano to be a two stage move, not five. We have already seen how the thumb move is the first stage. After that, the trick is not to then think of moving your 2nd finger to its new position, then your 3rd finger to its new position and so on. Instead, immediately your thumb plays its new note, the rest of your hand should move into its new position in one movement. This subtle difference is again designed to minimise movements and put good habits in place now that will serve you well later.

If you want to check if you are managing this successfully, play through this series of patterns where the last note each time is changing, and no matter which finger you need to use after the move, there should not be any delay because your whole hand has changed position in one movement:

C D E   F   G
1 2 3   1   **2**

C D E   F   A
1 2 3   1   **3**

C	D	E	F	B
1	2	3	1	**4**

C	D	E	F	C
1	2	3	1	**5**

Whilst all of these moves have involved you using your 3rd finger as the 'pivot' to allow your thumb to move underneath, we also very commonly use the same technique with your 4th finger as the pivot. In fact, whilst I am not here to convince you to practice endless scales and other exercises unless you really want to, getting competent in at least one scale pattern is definitely a good idea, and all you need to do is to extend slightly what you have already learned:

C	D	E	F	G	A	B	C
1	2	3	**1**	2	3	4	**1**

Notice that we could call this a group of three notes followed by a group of four notes. Then, rather than finishing on the final C with our little finger, you can simply pivot from the 4th finger on the B then you can start again. At which point, watch as the whole keyboard opens up as the pattern can just start again! Suddenly there is nothing stopping you going as far as you wish up the piano, because you can pivot from both your 3rd and 4th fingers. As before, it may feel like quite a long way to get your thumb underneath your 4th finger to get to the next note up the keys, and you may be tempted to twist your hand slightly to help. But remember, your thumb can touch the base of your little finger with your palm facing you, so there is no need for this twist, and with a little practice you will soon get used to it. Just remember not to flap your arms like a chicken!

A note of reassurance: when you get so that you are comfortable doing this manoeuvre from both your 3rd and 4th fingers, doing it with your

2nd finger as a pivot will seem easy! We do use our 2nd finger in this way in piano playing, but you will be pleased to know that there is NEVER any need to use your 5th finger (little finger) as a pivot, as it is not possible to get your thumb up to the next note without twisting your hand and flapping your wings and we do not want that!

The other half of the story (The game changer part 2)

Now that you have seen how to get all the way up the keyboard with your right hand, the other half of the story is obviously to find out how to come back down again in a similarly smooth fashion. Whereas before you used your 3rd or 4th finger as a pivot and brought your thumb underneath, now you are going to reverse the process. To come back down the keyboard, your thumb becomes the pivot and your 3rd or 4th finger comes over the top of it. Again, the crucial parts of the move are for your hand not to twist anticlockwise or for your arms to leave your side like a chicken flapping! Therefore, coming down the keyboard with your right hand will look like this:

C	B	A	G	F	**_E_**	D	C
5	4	3	2	1	**_3_**	2	1

As you will see, when you reach your thumb for the first time, your middle (3rd) finger comes across the top. Then if you wanted to continue coming down the keyboard, you bring your 4th finger across your thumb and the pattern can start again. As always, do not panic if this takes a bit of practice to get used to, just focus on keeping everything in a straight line and taking advantage of your thumb's natural sideways movement. Also feel free to try this process on any notes you wish on the piano, you do not need to worry about playing 'wrong' combinations of notes at this point. All that matters is enjoying realising how succeeding at this one way of moving around the keys (or reversing it to come the other way) suddenly opens up the whole instrument for you.

Then, when you feel like you are getting the hang of things, it is time to try the same process with your left hand. Obviously as your left hand is the opposite way around to your right, your thumb is the pivot to go up the keys, and your 3rd or 4th finger forms the tunnel for your thumb to come underneath coming back down, i.e. the opposite way around to how it works for your right hand. Take your time, work through it one stage at a time, and you will see how useful this skill is. Then, if you are feeling a bit ambitious, instead of trying these patterns with notes that are right next to each other, spread your fingers out and feel free to try them over a larger range of keys. Yes, some may be harder than others, but the principles of moving around the keyboard are the same so do not be afraid to have a go. Also, never forget that when you think you can play even a few notes or a basic exercise, to then try and do it again without looking at your hand. Every single time you try this has a benefit in the long run so it is worth it.

Where things get really exciting

In order to give you a range of patterns to try at first so that you do not get bored of doing the same ones, let me introduce you to one more shape, that can quite quickly make you feel like you are really getting somewhere. There are occasions where we use the word "chord" in music to refer to just two notes at the same time, but more frequently we use the term to refer to three or more notes at once. You will also hear musicians use the word "triad" which, it will come as no surprise to learn, specifically refers to a three-note chord. In many ways, these groups of notes are one of the most fundamental building blocks of how the vast majority of music is constructed, regardless of era or style. Whilst there are many different chord shapes, let us get you playing the most frequent, and certainly the most useful for a beginner to learn.

Return your right hand to the keyboard, again with five fingers over five consecutive notes, and instead of just playing one or two notes at once, I want you to play fingers 1, 3 and 5 at the same time. If you have put your hand in the same position as where you started the other exercises, you will be playing a C, E and G.

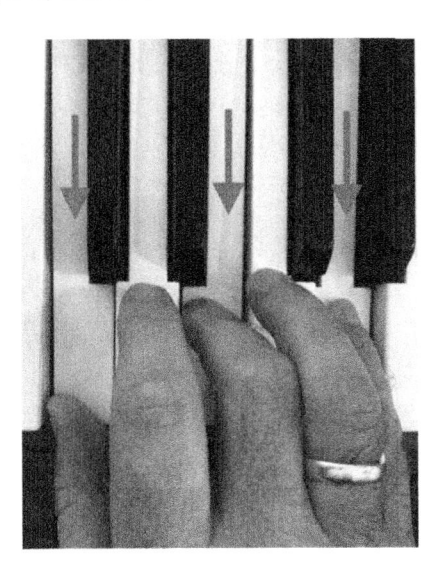

As before, this new shape may take a little bit of getting used to, especially in the case of knowing what to do with your non-playing fingers (i.e. 2 and 4). If you find that they are somewhat exaggeratedly pointing out of the way, or alternatively catching keys you do not want them to, do not worry that it is just you - it is not. Again, with some little and often practice, you will soon find that this shape becomes second nature. It is also worth saying that many beginners find playing this three note shape a little easier than playing the two note pattern outlined before.

Once you feel that you are getting a little more confident in this shape, and that you are striking the notes a little cleaner, I want you to try and take the shape and move your whole hand one white note to the right, i.e. if you started with playing your first chord shape with a C, E and G, you will now have moved to a D, F and A. Once you have done that, try moving back down to the chord you came from, then practice moving backwards and forwards between the two. As before, when you feel that you have improved a bit, allow your brain to focus on what this FEELS like rather than what it looks like, and try it without looking at your hand. Then start trying to extend the pattern by going up three chords and back down, then up four chords and back down, and so on, again playing without looking when you are ready each time. Keep doing this until you have managed to play a total of eight chords up the keyboard then back down. Notice when you play the eighth chord, your right hand thumb will have reached another of the same note as you started on (what we call an octave higher). So, for example, if you start with a C, E and G, and play a total of eight chords, you will arrive on another C, E and G.

All the way through these chord exercises, there is one trick that you can do that will greatly improve your speed of movement around the keys later. As you move from one chord to the next, make sure that your hand is staying in exactly the same shape as one movement. If you slip out of shape as you move, and end up moving your thumb up a note, then your middle finger up a note, then your little finger up a note, you have completed three physical movements when one (just moving your whole hand in shape) would have done. Whilst these are admittedly very small movements, and you may well be playing quite slowly at this point so it will not matter, if you can get into the habit of streamlining your movements around a keyboard now, it will hugely improve your chances of playing quicker later on. And if you can get to the stage where you are doing this looking at your hand as little as possible, you will be flying!

When you feel comfortable in moving this chord shape around the piano in your right hand, we are going to add one more simple thing which I promise you is for many people, a very special moment. Not only will you be starting to play different things with your two hands, but it suddenly starts to sound just a little bit more like music rather than an exercise, and I often refer to it as the equivalent of the moment when you first rode a bicycle without your supporting stabilisers: it is a little bit of fear and a lot of excitement all rolled into one, so here we go with the piano version!

All I want you to do is to get your left hand and return back to the very first exercise that you did, i.e. lie your little finger over a C towards the bottom of your keyboard, and put the rest of your fingers over the notes next to it so that you are covering from C to G. Then get your right hand over the same batch of notes somewhere around the middle of your instrument. With your left hand all you are going to do is play the C with your little finger. In the right hand I want you to play the first chord shape you have just been practicing, i.e. a C, E and a G, meaning between your two hands you are now playing 4 notes.

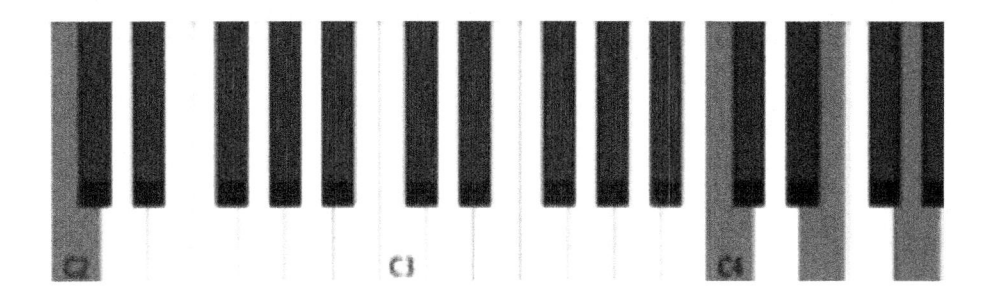

Your left hand is playing what we call the "root" of your chord in the right hand, i.e. the note that has given the chord you are playing its name. This obviously is not a music theory book, so I do not want you to worry about naming the chords at the moment (although if you would like me to take you from a complete beginner to an expert in music theory in 65 short video lessons, you can get lifetime access to my Read The Dots course bundle on how to learn to read music here: https://thatpianoguy.club). For now, it is enough to learn the concept of a chord having a root, and that your left hand is playing the root of the chord you are playing at the same time in the right hand. Notice how by adding that single note down the lower end of the piano, you have created a much 'fuller' sound.

Next, I want you to start moving the right hand chord one chord to the right (so to D, F and A, then E, G and B and so on), and each time you move the chord, you are going to play the chord's root in the left hand. So when your right hand plays a chord of D, F and A, play the D in your left hand and so on. Go up through five chords in total (and their individual single note roots in the left hand) then come back down. If you feel a little bit more ambitious 'dot about' in the five chords rather than playing them in sequential order, and notice how this starts to feel just a little bit more like music than an exercise. If you feel REALLY ambitious, rather than stopping at five chords, keep going until you have played eight (you will need to employ the sleight of hand trick I taught you earlier in your left hand, using your thumb as a pivot and bringing your third finger over the top).

Then, no matter how easy or difficult you have found that, or how far you took it, I want you to stand up, smile and give yourself a round of applause! I am serious! You have just taken a HUGE step on your piano playing journey and you might not have even realised. Why? For one very important reason.

Your right hand was moving up and down the keyboard, whereas your left hand stayed still and just changed which finger it was using. And that, ladies and gentlemen, is hand independence. To be able to move one hand to a different area of the piano and for the other one to NOT copy it and try to move too, is MASSIVE. This is the patting your head and rubbing your tummy at the same time moment. Our hands are so used to working together as a team, that conquering this autopilot tendency in the name of them working entirely independently as a piano player is a big step, and you just did it.

If you could feel your brain cogs struggling as you did it and it felt completely alien, please do not worry, and how many times have I said that in this book? At each stage, it might feel a bit weird, then with little and often practice it will gradually improve, and as I have said throughout, the best way forward is to keep doing a little bit then do it again without looking. Rinse and repeat. You have got this.

CONCLUSION

When you picked up this book, it is likely that you fell into one of several categories. Perhaps you were someone for whom playing piano had always been an idea, a vague thought of something nice to do, or something you had thought about for years but never done anything about. Let's be honest with each other here (I consider us friends now) you might have been the kind of person who has told people at parties you always wanted to play piano but never followed up on your dream. Perhaps you do that a lot? I don't know!

Or maybe you were someone who genuinely felt that there were reasons that stopped you being able to fulfil your dream of sitting at the piano and playing the music you love. Whether these were reasons of circumstance from when you were a child, or your current life situation, perhaps you thought that there were legitimate obstacles that meant this simply was always destined to be a pipe dream. Maybe you had even accepted it, no matter how disappointing.

Perhaps there were some of you who were actually motivated to make getting started on the piano happen for you, but were overwhelmed as to what your first steps should be. It is the same when you buy anything for the first time – you do not know what you do not know, and any new marketplace can be intimidating. Maybe it was not knowing who to ask, where to turn for tuition, what content was reliable information or what options there were out there that was stopping you. Whatever your starting point was, the reason you are here is that you have an itch that you want to scratch where the piano is concerned, and now that you have made it this far, the question I want to ask you is "What now?"

The early 2020s was a period that taught many of us a lot of important lessons. We all had some extremely unusual experiences during that time, and many people were put under an exceptional amount of strain both personally and professionally. One of the resulting effects of the Corona crisis was that an increasing number of people began looking for something they could do to relax and to improve their mental wellbeing, ideally from the comfort and safety of their own home.

Within the first month or so of the Corona crisis my online client base experienced incredible growth, as the number of members more than tripled! For many, it did not matter that this was not something they would quickly become experts in, it was a way to lose themselves for a short period of time, to switch off from the outside world, and have some time just for them. One member called Alwyn, commented on my LinkedIn profile that my course is, "Worth every penny. I'm loving it! Nothing made me happier during the height of the pandemic than putting on my headphones and conquering a song. This is stress free, travel free, judgement and expectation free."

I also think that unprecedented time caused a lot of people to re-evaluate what is really important to them. It made them realise that spending time doing something you truly enjoy, without it being directly related to the success of your career or your family, is a vital aspect of human experience. I think we have all found that sometimes we are all guilty of taking things for granted maybe just a little bit, and consciously taking decisions to try new things and sample new experiences without pressure or expectation, can only enhance the time that we have.

It has been so rewarding for me, as someone who has always had a passion for helping people to break down musical barriers and understand new things, to see how Piano Legends continues to help a growing number of people across the world to access being able to play their favourite music on piano. The fact that so many of them have, by their own admittance, been waiting many years to feel the excitement this gives them, is a huge thrill.

When you get comments like a lady called Lylie writing in our members community that, "I've been trying to learn this song on guitar for years and after 4 weeks with you I've made more progress than I could have ever imagined!!", you will understand what a smile that brings.

Or the kick I got when a member called James posted, "I've hit the big time ... I played hooks from 3 songs from memory and my family recognised them! This is what it is all about!" Great stuff!

Then there's a member called Sue who had been convinced she would never play for years, but soon after joining my course posted a video in the community where she wrote simply, "I think I finally cracked Elvis… YAY I LEARNED A TUNE!!!". I loved that one.

So, as we reach the end of our time together inside NOT Another Piano Book, it seems like a good time to ask you one simple question. It is a question I have asked many people over the years and will continue to do again whilst I share my passion for helping as many of you as possible.

It is an important one so take a deep breath, pause for a moment, and ponder this:

If not now, when?

Thanks for reading.

Mark

Here's that special offer

As a thank you for supporting my first book, if you are ready to dive into the magical world of piano playing for yourself, I would love to offer you a special offer on my Piano Library right now.

Inside you get access to a huge video library of content and courses, a collection of beginner courses, 4 song tutorial libraries from beginner to advanced (all laid out in a suggested order), optional support from and direct access to me and loads of great bonus workshops, extra mini courses, and lots of recordings of me playing too for when you fancy a chill-out!

And most importantly, as I mentioned earlier in the book, with Piano Legends you can add direct access to me inside our membership community to support you at every stage. Ask questions, post videos of your playing for personalised feedback, and have me as YOUR piano teacher.

As a special thank you for buying this book, and to try and make piano as accessible as possible for everyone, I am offering you a huge saving on Piano Legends with a 30% discount code off a one off purchase.

To unlock this deal...

1. Go to https://markdeeksmusic.com/piano-legends/
2. Click the button to join
3. Choose One Off Purchase
4. Enter the coupon code **PIANOBOOK30** to your shopping cart
5. Start playing the music you love right now

I can't wait to see you inside.

Websites

https://markdeeksmusic.com
https://thatpianoguy.club

Social Media Links

Please connect with me here:

Facebook
https://www.facebook.com/MarkDeeksMusic

YouTube Channel
https://www.youtube.com/c/MarkDeeksMusic

LinkedIn
https://www.linkedin.com/in/mark-deeks/

TikTok
https://www.tiktok.com/@markdeeksmusic

Instagram
https://www.instagram.com/markdeeksmusic/

Twitter
https://twitter.com/markdeeksmusic

BIOGRAPHY

I want you to know that when I tell you that I believe that anyone can get started playing piano, that's the voice of experience talking. I've been working professionally as a musician since the age of 15, which frighteningly is now more than 30 years ago. In that time, I've performed, taught, directed, composed, arranged, improvised, talked about and recorded in such a wide range of musical scenarios and styles, sometimes even I laugh to myself at the variety of how my career has panned out.

For example, for more than 25 years I have worked as a musical director and arranger for numerous community singing groups and choirs numbering anything from 3 to 300 singers on stage at once. Since 2018, I have had my own community singing company called Sing United, and we currently have more than 100 singers having also set up our own charity, the Sing United Foundation. These singers are just ordinary people like you and me, who sing anything from classical music to music theatre, pop to heavy metal, just for fun. And speaking of heavy metal music, I have a PhD in it (yes, really), am in two signed metal bands called Winterfylleth and Arð, and the 2020 Winterfylleth album 'The Reckoning Dawn' went into the UK Rock and Metal charts at number 7. Life is pretty varied.

I'm also a TedX and international speaker and workshop facilitator for businesses who want to use music to improve the wellbeing, mental health, creativity, engagement and performance of their staff.

I have taught British comedian Lenny Henry piano, worked as a musical director with Faye Tozer of Steps fame, and conducted the Royal Northern Sinfonia orchestra on several occasions. As I said, things are pretty varied. I have run choir projects for BBC, Metro Radio, and artists such as Lindisfarne, but then have also written string parts for Japanese rock band MONO. I have done orchestral arrangements of the music of Finnish heavy metal stars Sonata Arctica, have worked as a musical director on shows like West Side Story, and co-written a comedy musical with the BBC's Alfie Joey.

Did I mention things get pretty varied?

Amongst all this, I have taught countless people to play the piano. And I believe from the bottom of my heart that I can help you too.

Let's get started.

Printed in Great Britain
by Amazon